GAMES
LAWYERS
PLAY

GAMES LAWYERS PLAY

and Clients Too

DAVID M. COOK J.D.

Games Lawyers Play…and Clients Too
Published by White Tiger LLC
Denver, CO

ISBN: 978-0-692-12033-0
LAW / Essays

QUANTITY PURCHASES: Schools, companies, professional groups, clubs, and other organizations may qualify for special terms when ordering quantities of this title. For information, email David@KlanckeCook.com.

WHITE TIGER LLC

To the women and men who practice law
in a manner that moves them forward
on their path of life's higher purpose.

CONTENTS

INTRODUCTION

*H*_{e was lying to you}, I said reading with my head down, half listening to her lawyer story in the background.

Both of our heads came up at the same time and our eyes met – hers with a look of intense questioning and disbelief. I felt shock; I could not believe what I'd just said.

Imagine yourself alone at home at night. You hear a noise upstairs, and while not believing it actually is anything, you grab a kitchen knife and go to investigate. You turn on the hall light, now the only light upstairs, and notice that a bedroom door is closed, which is not normal. You open the door and see a figure holding a knife staring at you from across the room. As you stifle the urge to cry out, you realize that you are looking at yourself in your daughter's full-length mirror on the opposite wall. That moment of realization, that I was the figure with a knife, was how I felt as I looked into my client's eyes. Should I leave the room and regroup? Lie and say that I never said it? Admit that I said it but I really meant something else? These were all options. But I could not. I kept thinking about how I was looking into my own eyes in that darkened room. So I went ahead with the truth.

We had just finished a discussion about her estate plan and I was looking down making notes about her wishes. For no apparent reason she begin to tell me, as I wrote, of her contact with her lawyer on another case. Let's call him "George." She said that she had gone in to see George about six weeks ago and had heard nothing back from him. So she called him to see what was going on. She described how initially she felt lucky at being put directly through to him, but as they began to talk she noticed that he only discussed her case in very vague terms. George could not say anything specific about the case or its current status. He seemed preoccupied and rushed. She told me that by this time he was supposed to have taken certain actions, but in the conversation he was not able to say whether he had taken them or not. George said that all was going well. He needed to look a couple of things up and would call her back in a few days. It was at this point and without truly thinking that I looked at her and said, *He was lying to you.* Had I been paying attention to our conversation, instead of "on background," I never would have put it that way. I might have said that he was not telling you everything or used some more socially passive words. I probably never would have said anything. Most lawyers will leave a client's relationship with another lawyer alone unless that other lawyer is doing something really bad to the client. That was not the situation here. George was just offering up a run of the mill, cover-your-ass lie.

On some level, perhaps out of professional courtesy, that whole interaction was between her and her other lawyer. I had no reason to believe that George would not do a good job for her or even whether he really was less than honest during that telephone call. So why interfere? Professional courtesy is, after all, about allowing colleagues the benefit of the doubt. It was not my business to tell George's clients how he should be running his. Maybe George was late to pick up his daughter from soccer; maybe he just had a bad conversation with another client or with an intractable, aggressive lawyer and his mind was still wandering or processing the aspects of that case. Lawyers should probably hold their calls when they are feeling distracted or need to concentrate on some other job, but that did not give me any excuse to call George out. Since my client was background and I was on autopilot, I simply spoke without thinking or analyzing. George and I were busily engaged in the same fault: neither of us was really focused on the client that day. We were both on autopilot; he lied and I called him out on it. Either way, we both failed professionally.

But now it was out and there was no retreat. I considered my options, which included lying, of course. But I did not lie. Instead, I decided that she was my client, too, so I might as well tell her what I thought. I said, *From the moment you told George your name he did not have the slightest idea who you were or what your case was about. He was well aware of that, and while you were talking during the early parts of the conversation he was trying desperately to place you. He did not want to admit that to you so he pretended that he understood the situation but just needed a little more time to get back to you. He played 'make believe' that he was very busy but would get back to you soon.*

Lawyers are always 'very busy.' It is how we live and we love it. Even when it is not true, we love to put up that front. We love our little drama of constant crushing commitment. It doesn't help that George probably had no idea who the hell you were and just wanted to gracefully get you off the phone so he could have his assistant locate your file and he could, after waiting an appropriate number of days for 'research,' call you back and talk intelligently. Also, if he could buy a couple of days after the conversation, he could actually do some of the things that he had said he would do six weeks earlier and call you back, not only talking intelligently but presenting himself as on top of the case. George knows that one of the benefits of being perceived as perpetually rushed, busy, or simply an 'in-demand' lawyer is that the client will not get upset for another week or two when she doesn't get a communication, even if George said that he would call within 'a few days,' whatever that means. The client normally doesn't have nerve enough to say, 'Did you actually do anything before I called you?' She just thinks it. And George certainly won't bring it up.

At this point, my client was starting to understand.

I am not saying that you should quit him and find another lawyer. He may be a very fine lawyer, you just caught him by surprise and he felt that he had to be evasive. He was probably rushed, either just coming in or leaving, and took your call on automatic. Another time he might have screened your call, heard your name, realized that it was somewhat familiar but not immediately identifiable, and had his assistant bring your file. Then he could have much more convincingly distorted the status of your case. In a situation like yours, a quick look at the records on his laptop would not have been a great help because nothing had been done on the case. Alternatively he could have taken a message and either called you right back, or better, actually done something on your case first, and then returned your call the next day with the news of his accomplishments. Again, you would be too polite to call to his attention that he probably did that work in the last twenty-four hours, not four weeks ago like he should have. But you would feel good that something was done on your case, and he would feel good that something was done on your case, and you would both move on. In this instance, the evasion is still there but has become something subtle and acceptable at the same time, a new common ground from which to move forward.

In a moment of devastating charm and innocence my client simply said to me, *Do you think he will bill me for that conversation?*

I said, *Of course, he has to. He is relying on the fact that you both pretend.*

Lawyers have always banked on our clients' polite ignorance. You see, dear client, most of you do not have the nerve to confront us when we procrastinate and obfuscate. And we know it. We'll use this fact as a shield, if not a sword, whenever we need. Even those of you who do have the nerve do not know quite how to call us out and you fear losing us. Calling another person a liar is heady stuff, even for kids and teens. Doing it to a professional, much less a lawyer, is just never done. This is true even if the accusation is unspoken and stalking close to the surface of a conversation.

And the truth is that we will quit. Our final ace is our professional ethics. If you do actively confront us, it gives us a perfect excuse to simply get out of the case without admitting or denying anything, offering that *If you feel so strongly, we simply do not get along and cannot work together anymore.* It is a bit like those SEC settlements where the guilty party need not admit liability. But such a dramatic separation almost never happens in practice. You will not say what you really feel because of who we are, because of your investment both financially and emotionally in us, and most importantly, since much of what we do is magic to most people. The law is a complete mystery to many and clients fear that they might be wrong. Why risk the relationship with your lawyer? Of course, as our clients compound their bad experiences, they just begin to suspect that all lawyers must behave this way, at least when they have fallen short in performance.

Finally, (and bless you dear clients for this) you always hope, sometimes against all reason, that it will get better and that we will change. In this respect, working with your lawyer is like any other unhealthy relationship: the unrealistic hope against hope that the mere passage of time will cause another person to change for the better. But then how often do we try the same thing over and over, expecting something different *this* time.

After my client left, I leaned back in my chair in the conference room, put my feet on the table and reflected on what I'd said. I felt a sense of awe, but not over the conversation. After all, once the words spilled out of me, I really had nowhere else to go but with the truth. Instead, the awe was that I subconsciously recognized the deception so truly and without even consciously analyzing it. She really had no idea that her lawyer did not know her from Adam. And I knew exactly what her lawyer had pulled. After all, we all did it. It was one of those little games that any professional might play.

I never said those words again to another client, but I began to mentally catalog the games lawyers play. I played them myself, I heard about them in conversations with other lawyers, I even asked my clients and friends to tell me about their experiences. I did not use the words "games" or "deceptions" as such. I phrased my questions around difficult or frustrating experiences people had with their lawyers. Sometimes I'd simply ask, *Have you had experiences with your lawyer that left you feeling 'uneasy', but you could not put your finger on why?* Most times people had not understood what had really happened, so I worked to avoid embarrassing anyone. After all, I was a party to some of these games and I did not want to risk offense or trust.

This book is a collection of just some of these games that lawyers play with clients and with each other. I'm always hearing new ones, and they are as varied as the human situations that they represent. Yes, some of them are games I have played, but none of them rise to the level of malpractice. In fact, after I started cataloguing them, I found I got better at avoiding them. But these games can have consequences, and they are bad, maybe worse than some malpractice suits. They strike at the soul of the lawyer and of the profession. They raise fear and distrust in the client. They may break no law or rule of professional conduct, but in our heart of hearts we know what is going on and it hurts.

I once attended a legal seminar given in Colorado Springs, Colorado, by a highly talented and respected litigation lawyer. Most legal seminars are painful but his was excellent. At one point, he looked at a room of about seventy lawyers and asked to see the hands of each person who would get out of the practice if they reasonably could. About twenty-five percent of the participants raised a hand. The response surprised him. I assumed his surprise was that the number was high. He said he was surprised because the number was the lowest percentage he had ever seen in response to the question. He gave this presentation around the country and usually a minimum of fifty percent of participants raised a hand. In fact, he had been in large cities east of the Mississippi where seventy percent of people raised a hand. Then he said, *Do you know why you would get out if you could?*

No one answered.

You have heard the expression, "Holding an audience in the palm of his hand." I felt that experience. He held every lawyer in the room in the palm of his hand. The silence was profound.

He said that if you went to any freshman law school class and asked them to shout out why they were there, most of them would say that they wanted to see justice served, help others, help the poor, make the world a better place, and so on. You would not hear anyone say that they wanted to foreclose on people's homes, litigate divorces, or collect bad debts. Yet five or ten years down the road, these same young students find themselves working mostly on that second list. The games that lawyers play are deep reflections of this hurt and represent the struggle to deal with this hypocrisy.

I do not seek to criticize lawyers. Instead, I hope that this book is helpful to the profession. If a person's bent is not toward medicine, then I can think of no better way to make an honorable living while in service to others than the practice of law. Abraham Lincoln was a lawyer. Louis D. Brandeis was a lawyer. Francis Bacon was a lawyer. William Jennings Bryan was a lawyer. Calvin Coolidge was a lawyer. J. William Fulbright was a lawyer. Mohandas K. Gandhi was a lawyer. David Lloyd George was a lawyer. Alexander Hamilton was a lawyer. Patrick Henry was a lawyer. Andrew Jackson was a lawyer. Thomas Jefferson was a lawyer. Daniel Webster was a lawyer. Adlai Stevenson was a lawyer. Alexis de Tocqueville was a lawyer. All of them were great human beings and lawyers.

The pages that follow illustrate some of the games lawyers play. Every incident in this book is real or an amalgam of real events and people.

DISSOLUTION

Dan and Diane were high school sweethearts. Dan was a senior and Diane was a junior at Southwest High when they met. They dated steadily throughout Dan's senior year and through the following summer. It was a magical year and everyone said that they were the perfect couple. Even their names went together. Sometimes, without being too critical of their lives together, Dan and Diane both privately thought that the best of their relationship might have been that first year - right up until Dan went away to college.

At State Dan was surrounded by new people from all over the country. He was distracted, excited, and was meeting many interesting women. He and Diane went through a mandatory breakup in the spring of Dan's freshman year. They were separated for about six weeks.

Dan came home for the summer. After running into each other at the mall, they got back together. They pledged their love to each other but getting back together was also just the easiest thing to do. Just dating could be too "mean" and that described neither of them. Diane decided to go to State when she graduated later that year. They broke up one more time during their first year at State together when Dan started fooling around with a girl on the side. They tried to put it behind them with long talks and promises of future behavior. While doing so, Dan asked himself why was he dealing with the guilt of someone who was married when they were not even engaged?

Dan salvaged their crumbling relationship with an engagement ring. He had gotten back together with Diane owing as much to family pressure as anything else. Dan and Diane's families had become good friends and both thought that the kids were a great fit. Equally important, the in-laws liked each other and believed they could get along in deciding important matters like whose house do the kids visit for which holidays. To make matters more complicated, the word marriage was floating around long before Dan's guilt-ridden, apologetic proposal.

When Diane found out about Dan's infidelity, she called her mother. Diane's mother called Dan's mother who called Dan. No one knew it, but Dan's father had a brief affair when Dan was young. Though they happily reconciled, Dan's mother never forgot the hurt. And there was no way that she was going to let her son behave that way, married yet or not. She rehashed her emotional issues with him, talking to him of love, integrity and commitment. The conversation was cathartic for Mom. It was one she never had with Dan's dad and it helped for her to say things to Dan that she really had wanted to say to his father. She said that there would always be other pretty girls, and she did not want to see him start down the slippery slope that infidelity would surely lead him. She told Dan how much she knew he loved Diane. They did not need to be married for Dan to do the right thing in that relationship.

He had made a commitment and he needed to be a better man. Underlying this, as well, was the fact that Mom did not want the humiliation of admitting to Diane's mother the character failings of Dan. So in this conversation, both Dan's father and his girl-friend's mother were active participants through his mom's ego, but as a twenty-one year old boy, all he heard was an upset, nagging mother who needed to mind her own business. Of course, he could never say that to her face.

After thirty minutes of excoriation, his mother asked, *Do you still love Diane?*

Dan, of course, said, *Yes*. After everything, what else could he say?

Then you know what you need to do.

Over the years Dan often thought about that conversation. In hindsight, this was the moment, *that* moment. It is a funny thing about life: sometimes the moments that we assume are significant, like saying "I do" are really not that important. By the time you get to "I do," the choices have already been made, the roadmap has been locked in and the moment of actual decision remains somewhere in a jumbled past. Dan's moment came when he said "Yes" to his mother. After that, everything just happened. It was out of his control, and he resigned himself to whatever was coming. Not that what was coming was bad. Rather, that moment signified that what was coming was no longer primarily within Dan's control.

In later years, he would wonder how his life might have been different if he had had the nerve to tell his mother the real truth. The real truth was that, yes, he loved Diane, but he did not know if, at the end of the day, he wanted to commit the rest of his life to the girl he started seeing at seventeen. He had wanted to tell her off and make it clear that this was none of her business, but she was his mother. And he definitely cared for her. He was a good son and a respectful son, but no one seemed to be on his side. His father was the only possible person to help him, but Mom made it clear to him that, after his dad's personal failure, Dad did not have the moral standing to interfere in what she was trying to accomplish. Therefore, Dad did not interfere but secretly wondered if he was condemning his son to nothing more than a continuation of his own drama. Dan didn't "feel" wrong, but the message everyone was sending him was clear: this is the girl you are going marry. The perfect way to mollify everyone was with an engagement ring. As soon as he had managed to pop the question, he immediately became the family hero. The good news was that while he remained a little miserable inside, both families and Diane were ecstatic with thoughts of weddings and grandchildren and the eradication of infidelity in Dan's family.

Dan and Diane agreed to finish school before they got married. The families were anxious though, so once Dan graduated with his degree in business administration, they decided to have the wedding the following fall. The wedding secured, Diane saw no reason to go back to school. Dan landed a very fine job with a nationally known company after graduation, so she dropped out. When they got married Dan was twenty-three and Diane was twenty-two.

Dan decided, privately of course, that while he may have felt a little forced into marriage, he would not be forced into having children. Of course, the pressure started building fairly quickly. No one in the family actually confronted him, but everyone knew that he was the holdout on the question of children. Diane, on the other hand, saw motherhood as her real calling in life. When she left school and gave up on having a career, she intended children to become her outlet. She had been getting frustrated and started dropping not too subtle hints at the parents.

This might have gone on for a long time, but about three years later, Dan's father had a heart attack. It was a poignant reminder of the mortality of man, and Dan's mother wanted her husband to see the grandkids before he died, which Mom had no problem bringing up to Dan at the right vulnerable moments. So Diane gave birth to Marilou and then David, named after Dan's father, five years later.

Diane used her family powers of persuasion on Dan one more time to convince him that their two-bedroom apartment was too small for a family with two little kids, so they bought a house. Diane was pleased with her progress and status of wife and mother of preschoolers but once in a while she wondered what she had gotten herself into at the age of twenty-nine. She occasionally reminded herself of that sarcastic yet poignant phrase, "Be careful what you wish for, little girl. You just might get it."

By the time Dan decided to get a divorce, Marilou was in college. The kids' welfare had kept him from leaving, but now they were old enough that he figured they could handle it. He was ever more certain he could not bear the status quo much longer. He could not stand getting much older without changing something. He found the courage one evening when he was talking to Marilou. She said, *Why don't you just go ahead and get a divorce? David and I do not want it, but it is obvious to everyone that you are so sad and all you and Mom do is fight.* That conversation helped him greatly.

As he drove to the lawyer's office he kept wondering if he was in a dream. He would not have been in the least surprised to wake up at any moment to see Diane lying next to him, get up and go to work. But he is already awake. He is thankful that the lawyer's office is not far away from his job. He is just taking an extended lunch break for the appointment. No one knows except an old college buddy who recently got divorced and recommended the lawyer. Dan feels secure because neither the college buddy nor the buddy's ex-wife knew Diane.

But still Dan feels as if he is floating on waves of guilt. He can hear Diane's voice, he can hear his children's voices and he can hear his mother's voice. She was now in a retirement home in Florida and no longer exercises any real control over him. If the mother of his younger days were still active, he would never have the nerve to do this. The voices ring with questions and his every mentally verbalized answer is followed by an accusation or a threat by the voices. *You will be wrecked financially. You will never see the children. You will be disgraced before our friends and Diane's family. Your boss and people at work will think less of you because they all know Diane. The children will grow up learning that this is your fault and will hate you for destroying the family. Divorce is a sin. You will be shunned at church. You will have to find a new church, if one will take you.* Actually, of all the voices' threats, the one about Diane's family hurt as much as any. Dan genuinely liked Diane's father. He saw him as a friend and something of a father figure. They had their own little talks during holiday get-togethers and several times had gone fishing. If he went ahead, that would all end dramatically and forever. He knew that all the "I love you" and "We love you " talk that came from his in-laws was a particular kind of love conditional upon playing his role to their satisfaction. He was about to bungle his lines and exit stage right, never to return.

Dan found relief by hiding behind the justification that he was just going to talk to the lawyer to get some information and check out his options. At 43 years old, he was a successful businessman whose achievements resulted from always exploring his options before pursuing a direction. This was simply a business transaction and he was checking out his options. I mean, let's tell the truth, lawyers do not determine whether people are still in love or stay married; they simply handle the business part. That was all he was doing, checking out his business options. He may never get divorced. *OK voices, are you happy? Will you shut up?* They were not; they would not.

At a recent doctor's visit Dan learned that he was in excellent health. The doctor told him that if he kept going, he stood a great chance of seeing ninety. On the way home, Dan started to worry that the doctor might be right. Suddenly, and almost violently, Dan felt sick. He could not handle the idea of forty more years with Diane. For the first time in his life, he really thought that he would rather die than carry on in the marriage.

It was no one thing about Diane. Yes, he still loved her, but she dominated every aspect of his life. And it was a life that he had never felt any ownership of in the first place. She had to know about and comment on everything. In social settings people would ask him questions and she would answer. And while such behavior would seem to indicate that Diane held him in lower regard, at the same time she was extremely jealous. It was like his body was required to be present, but his personality was not. She made all the decisions and demanded all of his attention. There was a game they played that he hated. She would make up her mind on a course of family action and ask him for his opinion. If he agreed, it was over. If he disagreed the interrogation and dissection of his irrational thinking would begin until he gave up. Every other question to him began with "Why?" and his answer was never good enough.

Dan lived in a perpetual state of shame and apology, and most of the time he did not even know why or for what. Over the years he learned that loving someone may be the beginning of a marriage, but that alone was not enough to support it. Almost as important, you must like the person. He loved Diane, but had come to not like her.

Well, that was not exactly true. Years of bitterness and disappointment had left Dan internally disrespecting himself while remaining a seemingly respected person in his community. He was being punished for confronting his wife. He was being punished for trying to pull away from his family. He was being punished for living a lie for half his life. Forty more years? Dead in five sounded better.

And it was going to get worse. The kids' activities through school had given Dan and Diane common ground and something to focus on besides one another. What would happen when the kids were gone? In Dan's mind, that made it even more imperative to do something now. Waiting for the kids to grow up and finally move out on their own felt dishonest to them and to Diane. Plus he could not imagine coming home on that first night when they were truly empty nesters. He was afraid Diane would read his true feelings in his eyes. As long as the kids were around he could deflect that reality by focusing on their shared interest in the kids. But when the kids left, his countenance would reflect his truth. It might have taken him too long, but Dan had come to believe in direct honesty. People should not have to live lies. Plus, his talk with Marilou had helped push him to act.

Besides that, Diane would be much more likely to remarry and find happiness if she were single at age forty-two instead of age fifty-two. After all, Dan still had her best interests at heart. For goodness sake, he had spent his life so far trying to give her, and his mother, and her mother, what they wanted.

Misery has a way of driving around with people for a while,

and Dan did not take action immediately. At work, he heard some guys talking about divorce and they seemed to feel that the best divorce lawyer for a man was a woman. After all, women lawyers understood the opponent wife and could take the bitterness and redirect it. It was like having a spy in the enemy camp.

Dan was not sure about that. He wanted a guy as a lawyer just because he was done with women for a while and he harbored a secret fear that a woman would judge him for "abandoning his family," which a man would never do. Hell, the male divorce lawyer had probably already done the same thing himself. The two of them could just have one of those mutually knowing guy talks where not much has to be said. If the lawyer were a saint he would not be a divorce attorney. By the way, the reverse is not true. Women as divorce attorneys can be tough in the act of protecting their women clients from predatory men, whether husband or opposing counsel.

The guy recommended to Dan was Jon Slater. Jon was fifty and had been practicing law for twenty-three years. He started out as a high school English teacher, but he realized that he hated the constant meddling of the bureaucracy. And honestly, he did not feel like he could devote himself to the children the way other teachers did even though he liked kids. Jon started taking night classes and eventually earned his law degree. He never had any of the illusions about going to law school to do justice, help the world, help the poor, or any of that other crap that the younger law students thought about. He went to law school to escape a life as an English teacher.

He thought about becoming a prosecutor for a while and interned with some, but it just seemed like working for the school board all over again. Some but not a lot of respect, small salary, and even more work. No thank you. Eventually he got a job with a small firm that did divorce.

Divorce seemed like a perfect fit for him. Jon did not let things get to him. He had been a cool customer since childhood and his experience in the Air Force after high school taught him to maintain calm no matter what. That personality worked well in a field like divorce. Jon could keep emotional distance between himself and the crazy clients and the crazy judges and the crazy cases and, most of all, the crazy divorce lawyers. Jon could just compartmentalize the day, have two scotches and a bottle of wine in the evening, and be just fine. He was not a "bulldog" like some of the other lawyers wanted to be. He was calm and tenacious, and that worked. Jon also figured he would live longer that way.

After a while he struck out on his own. His practice was not too big and not too small, it was right in the middle. And while his practice diversified over the years, divorce was perfect for him. As he would say to his friends, *You do not have to be a Rhodes Scholar to do divorce.* The rules were laid out in detail in divorce law. Child support is a formula. Alimony is, more or less, a formula. Unless there is something really wrong with Mom, the kids live with her and Dad gets visitation. Divide up the marital property, more or less equally, and you are done. Even on simple cases, collect a $2,500.00 retainer up front (to be sure they are serious) and another $5,000.00 to $10,000.00 before it is over and you are good to go. Hire a couple of really sharp legal assistants and the practice begins to run itself. It was an unemotional formula, and the best lawyers were the ones who could keep themselves detached. That made Jon good at it.

Jon would be regularly surprised at social events when someone asked him how he could so casually divorce a couple, as if it were his decision. People wanted to know if he ever suggested counseling for couples. He did not. He frequently thought that the opposing attorney could use some serious couch time, if not drugs, but his client's state of mind was not his concern. The only counseling Jon suggested was for those clients who were so blinded by anger that they risked killing either one another or their lawyer. In truth, most people who have not been divorced cannot really imagine what life has become by the time they actually call him. By then, most couples are long since divorced in their hearts.

In contemplative moments, Jon reflected that neither the state nor the church actually marries or divorces people. He sometimes wondered when an individual arrived before her Heavenly greeter and proudly announced that she and her husband had a "successful" marriage of fifty years, would the greeter remind her that she despised him for the last twenty of those years and only stayed married by force of her religion? Does that still count as a fifty-year marriage or is it really only thirty, followed by a cohabitating de facto divorce for the final twenty?

Put another way; is the Almighty's awareness or opinions subservient to those of a state court divorce judge? Is He required to follow state statutes and a judge's ruling in deciding if a person is married or not? Is God free to make those decisions without being bound by the input of human institutions? This last one made Jon's head hurt and he did not like to think about it very much.

This simple perspective had a way of really shocking the sensibilities of people at cocktail parties. To Jon, divorce was better than spending life in a relationship that made one, or both, miserable; not to mention the self-deception of pretending to be married simply because the judge never ruled that you were divorced. Invariably, the next ethical inquiry he would have to face concerned the children. Why did he not encourage couples to stay together for the sake of the children? His reply was always the same and never satisfactory no matter how bluntly he stated it: the couple was already divorced in their hearts. The divorce did not take place when the judge said so. That was just the end of the legal relationship created by the state. What was the sense of propping up a crumbling house just because children are living in it? It was usually safer to get out; the kids were often better off with their angry, betrayed, and frequently vengeful parents living apart. People did not really like this answer, but it was the best one he had. And sometimes he was surprised to learn that the children were relieved. They were as tired of the screaming and the silences and the barely suppressed hate as everyone else. Jon did however always suggest counseling for any children under nineteen. They are, in fact, the only part of the divorcing family experiencing an irreplaceable loss.

The alternative was to stay married out of some sense of obligation to one's wedding vows. The whole process was such a mess because of the preachers, not the lawyers. The real deception was that people were expected to love one another forever. To Jon, this idea was insane. Even the happiest newlyweds had no way of knowing how long they could actually make things work, what the future would bring, how the in-laws would behave, or how money would affect things.

In Jon's mind, if a marriage were to stand any chance of success, a new vow was needed, a vow with some teeth in it, not just a platitudinous hope. The new wedding vow should be: *I will always tell you the truth about how I feel about you.* That called for a scary degree of honesty. Most people want their spouse telling them the complete truth about themselves in about the same measure as they want to tell themselves the truth about themselves. If people were just honest, they could manage all these issues with some dignity and not wait until things became poisonous. Jon thought about these questions a lot, but at the end of the day, he could not be overly judgmental. After all, he had been divorced, too, and that was after "trying to make it work" for two years too long.

At first Jon had wanted to keep it quiet because he thought it looked bad that he could not keep his marriage together. His friends ribbed him mercilessly. But once the dust settled, it turned out to be one of the best things he ever did. He learned more about divorce, divorce lawyers and divorce judges by going through the process than he thought possible. And it truly made him a better divorce lawyer. Working with another lawyer was an eye-opening experience. Sometimes calls got returned and sometimes not. If his lawyer was in court, days could go by before they talked. This inattention and casual involvement was infuriating and felt disrespectful - a fact that Jon carried forward into improving his own practice.

Notwithstanding his lawyer's laissez faire attitude toward communication, there was one form of contact at which he excelled. The guy billed like a machine. Also he billed in quarter hour segments. This may almost seem like a minor point but it can be powerful. A five minute conversation, and when talking to a lawyer a lot can be accomplished in five minutes, would always be billed as fifteen minutes. So, at $300.00 an hour, $25.00 worth of talk generated a bill for $75.00. It gets better, or worse, depending on which side you are on. If that lawyer can put one more five minute conversation with another client in that same 15 minutes, then he is making $150.00 for that time or an effective $600.00 an hour. Finally, when the lawyer returns all of his calls at the end of the day, one after the other, he can make exactly that happen. Jon confronted his counsel on that issue once and received the standard answer that the lawyer had to make notes in the file after the call ended and that took more time. Jon said to himself, *Bullshit*, knowing from experience that writing the note would take about 45 seconds. But the effect of this was that Jon only billed in one-tenth of an hour, six-minute increments, which seemed much fairer to the client.

When Dan arrived at Jon's office, Jon came out to meet him personally. His receptionist Lela was pleasant enough, but had a perpetually distant look in her eyes. Dan could not know that he was the fourth divorce that week, out of thirteen so far that month, making a total of one hundred fifty seven that year. After a while, they all kind of blended together. But this was Dan's first visit and it renewed the same mutual fantasy of wedding vows. Dan hoped for the magic of a clean and inexpensive divorce and Jon hoped for the magic of a sane client who followed Jon's advice and paid his bills without too much complaint. As in all relationships, there is compromise. After a few weeks, that relationship would turn into something else. Jon and Lela would get to know their clients in ways that sometimes surprised even them, and Dan would realize that he was simply in a business relationship with another human being, nothing more and nothing less.

Jon and Dan went in and closed the door to Jon's office. The privacy was illusory. They were going to replay the same conversation that Jon had with all of his clients. Jon and Dan chatted socially for a few minutes about the weather and sports. Jon always did that while the new client looked around the office and tried to size up Jon. The first 10 minutes of every meeting were always like this; Dan would be taking it all in and would not remember anything Jon said in any event. For his part, Dan wanted it to be clear that he was just testing the waters. He was not sure if he was really prepared to go down this road.

Jon smiled his most knowing smile. He understood. He also knew that by the time someone came to him, it was all over but the shouting. He listened to Dan's rationalizations and self-serving good faith: *I did everything I could.* Jon said to himself, *Really, everything? You did everything except tell Diane truth, tell your mother the truth and tell yourself the truth back when it counted and, candidly, before you had children.*

An hour and fifteen minutes later (and $350.00 lighter), Dan left the office. Jon was very helpful in helping Dan develop his perspective on the prospect of divorce. Dan was able to distill the process into those three magic words: *I am fucked.* He would have to pay child support until David was nineteen and maintenance to Diane for three to five years. She would likely get the home and at least half of their assets including Dan's retirement, and Jon suggested that Dan provide at least six months of grief counseling and therapy for Diane and the children. Jon explained that therapy helped people better manage their anger and hurt. This would result in a less crazy Diane, and hopefully, a more reasonable settlement.

A "less crazy Diane." Dan was not hopeful. Diane had managed to drive him into this corner just by being herself. As soon as she found out that he wanted a divorce, Diane was liable to show just how crazy she could be. And that was a scary thought. What he really wanted from Jon was for someone to tell him that, yes, he had every reason to go through with this. He wanted reassurance that it was okay to end his relationship. That the cavalry was coming to the rescue and Jon was the cavalry. And if none of this was the case, he wanted to know that, too. Dan would have paid a great deal for that answer, but Jon nicely dodged or threw the question back at Dan each time he asked. Jon had, after years of this, learned to stay the hell away from answering those questions. Each client had to live with his own decision and his own path, and Jon would not allow himself to become a pastor. He was just a lawyer.

Jon knew there were certain questions that could come back to haunt him in the following months.

Leila: *Jon, Dan is on line one.*

Jon: *Good morning, Dan.*

Dan: *Didn't you tell me . . .*

Finish that sentence any way you prefer, the conversation always goes to the same place of blame. Like most seasoned lawyers, Jon knew that even the slightest statement could be misinterpreted as a prediction of what the future might hold and was always remembered by the client as a promise, instead of an educated guess. Jon thought his list of professional referrals should include a psychic, if for no other reason, than to relieve that burden from him.

After the talk about the shrink, Dan thought maybe he should go see one for the answer, but he always viewed shrinks as pro-marriage compromisers. What he really wanted was someone to tell him clearly that it was okay to want a divorce. If it was not he would live with that. But either way, he wanted an answer. Dan figured that a "take no prisoners divorce lawyer" was much more likely to give him a cold, straight-forward reply than some wishy-washy grade school teacher who became a social worker who became a therapist who was always trying to "save the marriage." Saving the marriage, in Dan's mind, was equivalent to "taking Diane's side."

Dan went home and tried to put it all out of his mind. That evening, he and Diane planned where they would spend their two-week summer vacation. Diane wanted at least one week with her parents back east because they were getting old. As she put it, this "opportunity" may not come again. Dan very nearly laughed out loud. He did not really like his mother-in-law. After all, it was her call to Dan's mother so many years earlier that bound him into the marriage in the first place. He had lived through all the "opportunities" he needed. As he drifted off to sleep that night, the only thing he could think about was the expense of divorce. Could he afford to go through with it? He figured not, but he did not know what else to do. There was simply no way to just talk about it with his wife.

He woke feeling no better or resolved. Dan was occasionally capable of introspection when the mood hit, and he realized that he was being as crazy as Diane. He knew which way his feelings were taking him, but was not ready to take action. Divorce, he thought, should be like a 12-Step Program. At the beginning of each day, he should stand up and say, *My name is Dan, I am getting divorced and I am crazy.*

But crazy or not, it was the prospect of a visit with the in-laws that pushed him over the edge. The idea of seeing them, especially his mother-in-law, filled him with such dread that he thought he might be sick. Dan ultimately decided to get divorced in order to get out of the trip. The final straw was the strain of one more overly polite week with Diane's parents.

He told Diane and she seemed to take it well; she had suspected by his irritability and distance that something was coming. They agreed that he would move out of the house at the end of the month. The general courtesy of it all brought a scary sense of relief. Maybe they could just be friends, at least for the sake of the children? Maybe that friendship would even prevent Diane from financially punishing Dan? Maybe pigs fly, too.

After Dan went to sleep on the couch, Diane spent three hours sobbing on the phone to her mother. Diane's mom called Dan a bastard and suggested counseling. Thereafter, Diane's mother would never refer to Dan by name again. It would simply be *he* or *him,* or if she were feeling particular righteous indignation, *that son of a bitch.* She enjoyed the double whammy of the last one in getting at Dan's mother as well in one stroke. She always believed that Dan's mother felt her family was superior. Well what could she think now?

In any event, the next day, Diane's mother called Dan's mother who called her son at work as soon as she got off the phone. Without so much as a hello, she said, *I just hope to God that you are not having an affair.*

Dan remarked to the effect that Diane had helped curtail his interest in women. His mother just repeated the question.

Once convinced that her boy was not an adulterer, she confided that she had never believed Diane to be good enough for him. She went on and said that it had been Dan's father who really pushed for their marriage. It was because of his guilt that there had been so much pressure to do it.

Dan was immediately relieved at his mother's approval, even while he was frustrated over her true feelings about Diane. He had built his life around the assumption that she had expected him to marry Diane. Regardless, he made another appointment with Jon. After $2,500.00 dollars on the credit card, he was on his way. As he swiped the card he could not help but notice that Diane's name was on the card as well. It was not so much that he felt funny about seeing her name as that he realized that she could be swiping at a lawyer's office on the same card right now. He thought about how payment on the full debt would be handled in the future. Dan decided that he did not want to think about that.

To Jon, this case was like a thousand past and a thousand future cases. He liked Dan well enough, even if he was kind of a wimp who seemed too concerned about what wives and mothers thought. But that did not matter; Jon was getting paid and he knew he would do a good job. Diane's lawyer, Jenna, promptly filed motions for money and custody. The $2,500.00 retainer was pushed up to $7,500.00 and Dan was really in the thick of it.

Over the years, divorce law kept getting called something else. And every time Jon became aware of an ongoing social rebranding, he could not help but laugh at himself and his "career." When Jon first started practice, a divorce lawyer was called a divorce lawyer. Eventually, the title went out of fashion, and divorce lawyers started calling themselves domestic relations lawyers. Jon figured this was fine, assuming that "fuck you" constituted some part of the definition of a "domestic relations." Most recently, divorce lawyers had started referring to their job as family law. What a joke, he thought to himself. *I participated in the legal deconstruction of over seventy families last year.* If that was family law, then Jon was a great family lawyer.

No, Jon's practice had taught him the importance of being direct, and he still used the term "divorce lawyer." He liked its shock value. He wanted his clients to really understand, up front and without euphemism, what they were discussing. Hiding behind words like "relations" and "family" only served to blunt the impact of what was a pretty severe process. He also wanted clients to understand that, almost unique amongst legal practices, the result was guaranteed to be unpleasant. In a moment of black humor, Jon once proposed hanging that infamous warning offered to Dante over the door of his office: "Abandon hope, all ye who enter here." In every other area of the law, even criminal law, the client could legitimately hope for a happy ending. In divorce, it was always a case of cutting losses and making the best of weathering a downward spiral.

The most Jon could provide was the best possible financial arrangement for his client once their existing emotional separation was matched by a physical one. Jon was no shrink, and he knew from prior experience that to try and counsel clients through their troubles would lead to extra pain at the very least and at best would put him out his legal fees. Furthermore, Jon had his own alimony payments to worry about. So Jon accepted that his clients were emotionally separated already (assuming they had ever really been connected), and simply helped shepherd them through the physical and financial break.

While Dan stated twice to Jon that he still loved Diane, the side comments and passive-aggressive sniping made it clear that he also had a great deal of hatred and contempt for the mother of his children. In cases like Dan's, it usually started this way. By the time it was all over, he would have embraced his negative emotions and would only manage to keep them in check for the sake of the kids. Jon also knew that at the end there would be a part of Dan that would also hate him. Dan would hate Jon for playing a role in his inevitable humiliation and financial loss, for not getting Dan a better deal, for everything Jon was going to know about his personal life, but in particular for the humiliation. Our deepest negativity is always for those who cause or witness our embarrassment. And at $300.00 an hour, without any therapy, help, or compassion going back Dan's way, Jon had to be detached and honest just to make sure the bills got paid. In other words, Jon did not want Dan to be emotionally dependent upon him. Jon made a point to always call a divorce a "divorce," and continued by telling Dan up front how bad it was going to be. So when Dan made noises a year into the case about the final bill not being fair, Jon got to politely say, *I told you so.*

As the case progressed, Jon found himself wondering what Diane saw in Dan. The guy was a bit of a wimp who called constantly. At first the calls focused on his self-doubt around the whole process. Later, he would call to make sure that Jon was doing the right thing. It got to the point that Jon got tired of talking to Dan and frequently had Lela run interference for him.

Lela quickly got to the point where she could recognize Dan's voice even before he said his name. Dan tried to make friends with her in order to get more access to Jon, but that was not going to happen. Lela was a divorced single mother of two teenagers who had a standing date with two girlfriends for happy hour every Friday after work. The girlfriends loved Lela's stories about Jon's clients. Lela could put them into tears of laughter as she talked about the cases, and sometimes repeated the telephone conversations word for word with voice inflection. She tried to never use client names, but sometimes it was difficult to fully tell the story without some sort of description of the client for scenery and effect. Dan would have been surprised to know how much fun he provided to three ladies every Friday afternoon. Lela saw right through his efforts to be her friend, and she knew who signed her checks. Dan wanted to get to Jon, so all the charm in the world or pleas of distress were no help in getting past her. Dan was just another client, one of three this week, thirteen this month, 157 this year, thousands in a lifetime.

And so it went. Jon worked on the case, but carefully avoided playing therapist to Dan. He would usually call back after the second "please call" telephone message in three days. Jon knew he had to call to spare himself additional time wasted listening to Dan whine about Jon's lack of communication. Nor did Jon like inventing excuses that were intended to spare Dan's feelings. After all, Dan just wanted someone with whom to commiserate. Striking a balance between courtesy and not wanting to be bothered was a challenge.

Eventually Dan would call back and whine about how hard financially it was for him, or how mean Diane was and maybe the best thing he could do was call the whole divorce off and try marriage counseling. At least that would be a lot cheaper. Jon really wished that Dan would stop complaining and just say what he wanted. He married the wrong girl, and to listen to his story, knew it going into the union. What, exactly, did he expect his divorce lawyer to do about that? But the interactions were having one effect: Jon found himself hating the case and wanting less and less to do with it.

He never said this to Dan of course. In fact, it took a while for Jon to realize what was happening. At some point, Jon decided that Dan had to go, but he had to go in a way that kept him paying his bill and not filing a complaint with the bar association. Jon had already divorced himself in his mind from this client. All that was left was to sort out the property split. He hung up the phone resolved to find a way to settle the case.

The next day Jon ran into Diane's lawyer, Jenna, while at court. He pulled her aside and suggested that there was no point in having the clients spending great sums of money to try this case. He hoped that the two lawyers, as rational professionals, could come to a reasonable settlement for both sides.

Jenna was not that kind of lawyer. She smelled weakness, and smiling, said that sounded great. She would draw a proposed settlement, and suggested that they delay the mandatory mediation session. If she could get them to settle before that, it eliminated the risk of Diane getting less as result of professional negotiations. She went back to her office and immediately called Diane.

I saw Jon today and I think he is losing interest in Dan and this case. We need to get together and revise our wish list. I think they are getting tired of the battle.

Diane smelled retribution and vindication in the wind.

That night Dan called to talk to the kids. When they were finishing up, their son David made that fateful statement: *Don't go yet Dad, Mom needs to talk to you.*

Dan's heart dropped. He had been hoping to get off the phone without interaction with Diane. Diane always stayed close and listened intently when David and Marilou talked to Dan. It made her angry when she saw how nice they were to him, how solicitous of his feelings they were, how oblivious of the fact that she was the injured party, not him. A part of her (not very far below the surface) wanted her children to treat their father with the contempt he had earned. The fawning drivel that the kids spewed over the phone just made her unaccountably angry.

She took the phone, and with no small amount of satisfaction said, *I hear your lawyer is tired of you and the case.*

What?

Diane's eyes sparkled just a little as she explained. *My lawyer ran into your lawyer at court, and my lawyer thinks your lawyer is ready to give up on you. Looks like you had the same effect on him that you've had on everyone else in your life. My mother was right about you.*

She did not really listen to his response, but she hung up the phone with a sense of deep satisfaction.

A little later, Diane thought about a conversation she had with Jenna early on. Jenna had told Diane not to antagonize Dan, lest the process wind up derailed. Diane began her reply to Jenna with, *After what he has done to me…*

Jenna cut her off. She explained that the divorce would go smoother if Dan had no reason to drag his feet and if Dan had been a saint, there would be no divorce. (In other words, *I didn't marry him, stay with him for years, have two children with him, you did. You must have known how 'bad' he was early on. On some level you chose this and remained with it.*) Once they had completed the process, Diane could say whatever she wanted, but she should hold off until it was over. It might not have been the most immediately gratifying advice, but it was sensible.

The next morning Diane called Jenna and began the conversation with, *I may have made a mistake last night…*

Jenna finished the thought saying, *You told Dan that his lawyer wants to quit?*

Yes.

Jenna blamed herself. She had almost called Diane back after the conversation to tell her to keep their interchange private. She wished that she had.

Lela opened Jon's office at 8:00 a.m. but he did not arrive until around 8:45 a.m., unless he was in court. When Jon arrived the next morning he had one message in his box, from Dan timed 8:01 a.m., and marked "Urgent." Something told Jon not to blow Dan off on this call even though with every part of his being he did not want to return it. He took a deep breath and dialed.

Dan was angry. *Did you tell Diane's lawyer that you were going to fire me and quit the case?*

Wherever this conversation was going, Jon knew it was going to be ugly. A part of Jon achingly wanted to tell Dan the truth about how tired he had become of Dan and the case. Instead, Jon said, *No, why?*

I spoke to Diane last night and she said you did. Dan knew this was something of an exaggeration, but he liked the feeling of righteous indignation. In his relationships he so rarely got an opportunity like this. Besides, Jon had been avoiding him, and it felt good to call him out and have him humiliated for a change.

Jon told Dan about the conversation with Jenna the day before and tried to put a positive spin on it. After all, if they could reach a settlement sooner rather than later they could save an enormous amount in stress and attorney fees. That was what Jon had talked to Jenna about. Lawyers had talks like this all the time; backroom deals that sometimes saved enormous headache down the road. In just a few minutes Jon was able to turn the entire conversation around. Instead of wanting to quit, Jon quickly had Dan convinced that Jon just wanted what was best for his client.

Dan started feeling a little guilty. He completely agreed with Jon's assessment. After all, Diane had spent their whole life together manipulating Dan. It made total sense that she would find a lawyer who did the same thing.

Quickly thinking on his feet, Jon further analyzed what had taken place. This Jenna and Diane situation told him a lot about Jenna and how to fight this case. She had turned an innocent and good faith effort by him into a petty bid to prove her aggressiveness to her client. Why? Because Diane was looking for revenge. And clients frequently picked lawyers that seem to match their personality. Jenna wanted to impress upon her client that she could deliver an emotional victory early on.

At this point in the conversation, Dan was feeling better about his legal counsel and yet somewhere in the back of his mind he knew that he had lost the initiative with Jon. Dan had been ready to give Jon a piece of his mind, and here the guy had completely turned the situation around. Jon sensed it too and asked him to settle his overdue account. Dan agreed to pay $3,000.00 now and again next month. He even thanked Jon, not once but twice, for having returned his call so promptly.

As he hung up, Jon could only shake his head. At least he and his girlfriend were going to have the money for a great weekend in Aspen.

For his part, Dan went to work in a fog with that floating feeling again. He was emotionally unmoored. Somehow he still felt like there was something he needed that he was not getting. Only now, he felt like it was Jon who was the culprit. For all the emotional strain and pain he was going through, he still expected his lawyer to understand. He really wanted some sympathy from someone and everywhere he turned, he felt rebuffed.

Later that morning, Jenna's receptionist told her that Attorney Jon Slater was on line two. *That was fast…* Jenna knew exactly why he was calling, so she immediately apologized.

Jon was elated, another coup. Jenna never said she was sorry to anyone. Dan had actually brought him a couple of really nice, albeit small, victories today. Not to mention the prospect of a room upgrade in Aspen. For an encore, he acted a little wounded, just for a touch more leverage.

Jenna completely ignored his "wound." He clearly did not understand that she enjoyed wounding him. He got one apology and that was it. They still had mandatory mediation in two weeks, then a hearing a week later. This thing was running up everyone's bills, and she did not screw around where money was concerned. Jenna lived on the ball and did not give quarter to those who did not.

What do you think Diane will need to settle? As soon as Jon asked the question, he knew it had been in error. What he should have said was simply, *Tell me what you want.* He should have spoken a statement rather than a question.

Well, you know, she is really hurt. That is why she talked to Dan like she did last night. He left her with two children. She suspects he's seeing someone else. She dropped out of college just to be with Dan. Those three years of credits are now too old and are not transferable. She would like to get her degree in the psychology of communications and that will take about 7 years. After all, not only does she need to start from scratch, but also because of the kids, she can only attend part-time. Dan needs to take care of that. In short, she is very hurt and does not think she will ever get over it. Diane thought that she would be a Mrs. for life and that whatever problems they had were resolvable through counseling, which Dan refuses to even try.

Jon thought, *What is this, Oprah? Just give me some numbers.* Jon did not want to play this game any longer.

Jenna, almost as though she had had the figures in front of her, came up with set of beautiful settlement numbers that were calculated to be just about 10 percent higher than a judge would probably award. Jenna had calculated something that was not so high that Jon would have to reject, but it had to be high enough for Diane to believe she had won. Also she now knew the truth that Jon wished to be rid of Dan and would probably support a higher payment from his client.

Jenna also had intelligence on her opponent, and that was enough to leave her feeling very confident about the case. Three weeks earlier Jenna had called to speak to Jon. He had been out of the office, so she got a chance to talk to Lela. When Lela did not immediately recognize Jenna or the case, they tried to locate the record by the trial date, December 1st. Lela checked Jon's court schedule, and found that Jon did have a court appearance that day - with a different attorney named LuAnn.

LuAnn and Jenna, while not friends, had served together on the board of the Women's Bar Association a few years earlier. Jenna called her immediately and asked about her court appearance with Jon Slater. The case was in Jefferson County. Jon was representing the wife, and LuAnn the husband.

Any chance of settling?

None. We have been to counseling and mediation and there is no chance. Jon's client caught my client kissing his girlfriend in the parking lot of Costco. It's a big lot, what are the odds? After it all came out, she booted him out of the house and threw his stuff onto the lawn. There are no kids, but lots of property is on the line, and no one willing to be reasonable. Jon's client wants her day in court, spelled R.E.V.E.N.G.E.

Short of the death of one of the parties, my case is going to trial on December 1ˢᵗ.

That was just what Jenna needed to know. Many lawyers, especially in smaller firms, including Jenna, set multiple trials on the same day. After all, every lawyer knows that something on the order of ninety percent of all cases settle, and a lawyer could set two or even three cases for trial on the same date in different counties knowing that at worst only one will actually go to trial (usually). Jenna was no different. She had regularly set multiple cases for hearing on the same day and had only gotten burned once or twice a year. It was a little dangerous but it made sure the attorney had billable hours on the trial date instead of a day with no trial and no appointments.

In fact, Jenna had another case set for hearing on December 1ˢᵗ, but she also had an associate - someone who could take over in the event of a double booking that panned out. But Jon did not. He was a solo practitioner. When he set Dan's case for trial on December 1ˢᵗ, he knew that LuAnn's case was already set that same day in another county twenty miles away. Jenna had read about Mystics that could supposedly appear in two places at once, but she was pretty sure Jon was not one of those. He was planning for Dan and Diane's case to settle. In fact, he was counting on it.

That gave Jenna a massive advantage. She could play hardball, and as long she did not get really greedy, Jon would be the first to blink. That is how she came up with the settlement figure. Tacking on the ten percent was just egregious enough to be taken seriously, but not so greedy as to be ruled out. It was just on the punitive side of the financial zone, but not offensively so.

Jon hung up and decided to try to sell it, or some version, to Dan. But he had to sell it to himself first. Was it really worth considering?

As any trial lawyer knows, there is a 1 in 10 chance of something really unexpected and ugly happening in any case that could make that 10 percent seem like a great deal. The judge could decide she does not like Dan whether for being a whiner or for catching him in a lie or any number of other reasons. The division of property could become pretty lopsided in that event. Of course, the reverse could happen too. But that was unlikely considering all the circumstances. Appeals rarely go well in cases of divorce, and the trial lawyer could wind up running up another $20,000.00 with the ever- higher possibility of not getting paid. That would leave Dan right where he was, if not worse off.

In addition, Jon was already a little concerned that the judge in the Dan v. Diane case was underwhelmed with Jon. He did not know why he had this feeling, but it nagged at him. He also seemed to recall that the judge liked Jenna very much. They might have known each other from the Women's Bar Association. But Jon could not ask Dan to accept a high settlement just because of personalities. Jon observed that divorce judges were on the fringe of mental regularity as compared to other judges. All judges suffered from the myth of self-importance and the adage that "All power corrupts." But the divorce group seemed to have less immunity than most. Maybe they just got jaded from spending their lives listening to divorce cases after having spent their early lives as divorce lawyers. Regardless, Jon figured that with a whiny client, his own personality, and a judge that may have something against him, he had a real problem on his hands.

Besides that, it was crazy to take this case to trial. The offer was high but that could be negotiated. Dan would be better served by avoiding trial. After all, he could get on with his life, and child support would end after a couple of years. It did not seem unfair to help Diane through college, and Dan made enough of an income.

Hell, in a couple of years, Dan would probably marry some chick that was in grade school when he had married Diane. In a few years, he will have forgotten all about this. Diane will probably never remarry, but she will be taken care of at least.

And there were the kids. No matter how much animosity there was between Dan and Diane now, it would be irreparable if they confronted each other in court. The kids will be forced to know their parents tore each other apart, and would start demanding that they take sides. For their sake alone, Dan should take Jenna's offer. And frankly, when you added up the lawyers' fees for both Jon and Jenna for trial preparation, Dan might actually wind up better off. Still, Jon was naturally suspicious of anything that might make things too much easier as being unfair to his client.

D an broke pretty easily. But most guys did; men are generally terrified of seeing their wives in court. They only wear two faces, hurt or angry, and hurt has a way of turning angry very quickly. Both Jon and Dan surmised that Diane might very well be looking to the courtroom as a place of her own vindication and vengeance. Neither wanted that and Dan really did not want that. Dan gave up so easily that it reinforced Jon's belief that this guy was a wimp. In fact, he barely put up a fight. Jon did not point out that the figure was ten percent over the average settlement, of course. He simply said that it was in the normal range give or take. Jon walked Dan through most of the conclusions that he had reached about the case, but kept going back to attorney fees. Jon hammered the point home that even with a settlement, Dan was going to owe him another $5,000.00 and those numbers would just continue to skyrocket if they took the case to court. Because Dan was a businessman, Jon tried to explain all this in terms he might understand:

the divorce proceedings were not a good investment and the sooner they were terminated, the higher Dan's ROI. It was really just like selling a losing stock. They agreed that Jon would go back to Jenna with figures that were 5 percent over the likely court result.

As soon as Jenna saw Jon's letter she smiled. The war was over and she had won. All that was left was mop up. She considered staying tough and insisting on the 10 percent, but she had another case on the morning of December 1st, and she did not want to risk a double booking any more than Jon did. Besides, the other case was complex and Jenna was not certain her associate was up to it.

She immediately called Diane and asked for authority to go as low as 8 percent over the probable award. Jenna focused especially on the emotional toll that going to trial would have on Diane and the kids to strengthen her position. She also suggested that judges did not always award attorney fees to the wife and her bill was already $17,500.00 before the trial. Diane agreed to accept the settlement.

But Jenna was not done yet. She immediately called Jon and said that she was thinking that she could persuade her client to go to nine percent. Jon tried to act cool, but the fact was that he was simply happy this whole affair was behind him. In fact, he felt good about the job he had done - Dan was getting a better deal than he knew: a whole percentage point shaved off, just like that. Jenna promised to check in with her client and let him know.

She spent the rest of the day on other projects, and did not even contact Diane. There was, of course, no need. She would let Jon stew for a while, and once he was good and edgy, tell him the "good news." Jenna resolved to contact Jon the next day, sometime in the late afternoon. The only worry was Diane. If she started antagonizing Dan again, there was no telling what might happen.

When Jenna did not get back to Jon, he did indeed begin to stew and worry about the worst-case scenario. So at 3:30 the next afternoon he called Jenna to check in.

Of course! Jenna was breezy and relaxed. *My daughter had a basketball game and I just got caught up in things. Sorry for not getting back to you.*

Jon was not feeling quite as relaxed and simply pushed past the pleasantries. *Did you talk to your client about the settlement?*

Yes, and she will not go any lower than eight and a half. She is aching to look Dan in the eye in court, and she refuses to let him off any easier than she has to.

Well, said Jon. He felt slightly sick, and wished he had not made any promises to Dan, but he could sell that deal to him - Dan pretty much had no fight left in him. *I think we can work with eight and a half.* If it proved too hard to get Dan on board, maybe he could knock an extra $1,000 off of the attorney fees. That might even make him feel a little better about the whole experience with Dan.

Together, Jon and Jenna agreed that they would appear in court the following Tuesday morning to make a record before the judge and then follow up with a written settlement agreement. The only remaining hitch was that the judge had insisted in seeing the parties in person and confirming their willingness to settle before allowing the December 1st court date to be cancelled.

Both of their clients howled at the agreement. Dan raged that he did not want to be in the same room as "that woman." Diane was similarly miserable. She wanted to hurt Dan, but she did not want to be around him either. Both of them wanted to know why they could not just sign something and be done.

But the problem was not that simple. Because of the children and the level of animosity, the judge did not want to remove the case from the docket only to have it re-set for trial because someone backed out on a settlement they did not really want to accept.

Both Dan and Diane had reasons for not wanting to see the other. While Diane may have wanted to make Dan lose in court, once she had won she did not want the emotional storm of actually confronting Dan for no gain. In the child custody/visitation discussions, Diane had felt vindicated when she was able to get Dan's time with David limited to two weekends a month and only two weeks in the summer. When she realized that this left Dan completely free from family responsibility and with free time to do things like date and go drinking with his buddies, she started seeing her martyrdom a little differently. She also knew that, statistically speaking, Dan would re-marry within two years while she would likely end up single for the rest of her life. Somehow, by seeking to take everything she could from Dan, she had left herself in a situation where he lost money but gained his liberty at the expense of hers. Diane realized this mistake, and even if she did not say so, she did not want to see the newly available Dan. He had been working out, was looking pretty good and had a great job. He was a commodity that was in demand, while Diane had to carry on exactly as before, but with only half the help.

On top of that, her attempt to "win the hearts and minds" of the kids was backfiring. Because their time with Dad was so limited, the children adored and protected him. Absence truly does make the heart grow fonder, while familiarity breeds contempt. In fact, Jenna had warned her about this. If too many restrictions were placed on Dan's interactions with his children, or Diane spoke too harshly about Dan, or blamed him for the divorce (regardless of the truth), the children would be tempted to protect their father in his absence and eventually blame Diane for breaking up the family. Dad might have initiated the divorce, but the kids would perceive Diane as vengeful and mean.

Diane would hear none of this. She just wanted to win and prove to herself (and to her mother, who followed the case and interrogated/advised Diane on a daily basis) that she had triumphed in every way possible over that lying son of a bitch. Diane was no more rational than Dan in her pursuit of a marriage death with dignity, but her behavior had powerful repercussions into the future. All of that was condensed into the feeling she experienced when one of the kids answered the phone with a bright and cheerful *Hi, Daddy!* She wanted them to share her contempt, but it was not working that way. It was almost like the kids had emotions to consider and an independent relationship with both parents. But they should not. They were hers and she was the victim, not their father.

Dan was also pretty put out when Jon recommended that they acquiesce to Jenna's demand for the house and its contents. Because of the children, Diane would probably get the house anyway. This was about as good as it could have been because Dan still got half the equity. As far as the contents were concerned, Jon's reasoning had been that it was nothing Dan would really want. Everything would just serve as a reminder of their failed marriage. It was better to start fresh. *Take your golf clubs and the few things that are really, distinctly yours, and let her have the rest. Good riddance.*

Dan liked that advice and bought new furniture for his apartment.

And Jon was right on both sides. Diane soon realized that what had seemed like a major coup only served as a constant reminder of happier times when each piece was purchased together. She made up her mind that when she sold the house, *all that crap* would go.

Despite the reservations of both parties, the court date came and went without a hitch. Both attorneys and their clients were cordial. For the sake of the children, Diane kept a smile on her face, and Dan was so relieved he started to become almost chatty with her. Afterwards, Dan went out for a celebratory drink with friends. Diane went home and cooked dinner.

Dan did indeed remarry eighteen months later. He and his secretary even got pregnant and they started a new family together. Diane got her degree and became a business coach. What she learned while getting her degree helped her deal with her own emotions. While she could not quite forgive Dan, she did eventually understand the long view that she had pushed him into marriage and the rest. But she always had to fake a smile for Dan's new wife. She worried that Dan would leave the kids behind in favor of his new family, and so she started to insist that the kids spend more time with him. To his credit, Dan always spoke highly to the kids of their mother. His new wife did her best to be their "friend" but it never really took.

Lela made the mistake one Friday afternoon of dropping a client's name during her Friday night out with the girls. By incredible coincidence, the client's father was at the next table and Lela got fired. Jon did not want to fire her, and sorely missed her, but it was the only way to keep the client from reporting him to the bar association. These days, Jon drinks more and more, and wonders how he ever got into this practice. Unfortunately, he cannot get out of it because of the substantial monthly child support he still owes and he is not really qualified to do anything else.

Jenna took her friend LuAnn out for a special lunch on the day the court entered the final decree of dissolution of marriage. She never did tell her why.

LIFE AFTER MOM

Dad was supposed to go first. Everyone understood that, especially him. Mom was the healthy one. She worked in the garden, walked two miles with the neighbor three times a week, and watched her weight and what she ate. She was always nagging Dad about losing weight, getting exercise and cutting back on the fast food lunches and the occasional cigarette. Plus she involuntarily cringed when she went out with him and he would order the "senior coffee" or the "senior" this or "senior" that. She just felt weird about that. She thought that "senior" meant only your last year of high school. Getting old was fine for other people, especially folks on a fixed income, but she could not accept herself as a senior citizen. Being senior and acting senior were a bid for pity, an admission of surrender. Especially when all "senior" garnered was a quarter knocked off the price of a coffee.

When Dad protested that everyone his age was simply looking for a little well-earned break in price, Mom said, *That does not make things better, it makes them worse. This post-World War II generation should be focusing on helping the young people, not expecting special treatment. The twenty year old in school, the thirty year old with three kids should get the price break on coffee. Old farts like us have plenty of money.* She really liked the "old fart" reference. Dad just went blank and said to himself, *but all seniors expect and deserve it. Just look at AARP Magazine.*

Mom did not remember exactly when she started feeling the pain in her lower back. She noticed it while gardening and was able to cover it up with increasing doses of painkillers for a while. By the time things were unrelentingly bad enough that she went to see a doctor, it was too late to arrest her illness. She would live for another fourteen weeks, leaving the family in a state of numb shock from the time of her diagnosis. They stopped watching the zombie shows because it felt just like who they were.

Mom was great during those fourteen weeks though. She struggled a little bit, but did not start to fade until week ten. When the end came, she was only in hospice for three days. Before that happened, she devoted herself to her family and worked to bring them to terms with her impending death. She had had three kids of her own, four if you counted Dad. The kids dealt with things as best they could. It would be hard to go on without her, but they knew they would manage. Besides, someone needed to be strong for Dad.

Dad had a really hard time coming to terms with Mom's passing. Sometimes it seemed as though he blamed her for getting sick and abandoning him. He would say things like *How am I going to run the house without you?* or *What will the garden look like without you?* or *How can we have Thanksgiving without you* (meaning who is going to plan and cook)*?* At first, this was fine. Mom was flattered by his recognition of how much of the family life was dependent upon her. Mom would smile and squeeze his hand. But soon it became clear that he really did not know how to deal with his life after her death. He was scared, unsure, and really wanted guidance. Mom was dying. Truth be told she did feel a little annoyance that her few weeks to live translated into self-indulgent concerns for him. She felt a little lost and unsure as well. Eventually, she stopped responding and would simply leave him to his thoughts.

Around week five, Mom developed this positive attitude towards her death. Her new mantra, taken from Winston Churchill was, "I know that I am ready to meet my Maker, but I am not sure that He is ready to meet me." For the remainder of her time on earth, she stayed strong. In her final moments, she booted her husband and three kids - Sam, Lilly, and Randy - out of her hospital room so that they could eat and she could have a few minutes peace and quiet. Ten minutes after they'd walked out of the room, she closed her eyes for the last time and was one with the One once more.

She needed only a moment to get ready.

Two years went by. Dad was only sixty-eight, but Mom's death had changed him. He did not go out. He did not call. He did not lose the "going through the motions" feeling. It was not that the kids did not want to go see him; it was just that the house had started to smell like an old man lived there.

It looked like it, too. His house just seemed dark and gloomy. He had taken to leaving newspapers lying around and keeping the curtains drawn. It was not that Dad was unclean; he just would not bother to move his trash until trash day. He would sit in dusty sunbeams watching television and doing crosswords. The kids found it all to be a little morbid. Sam described it as oppressive. To help, the kids hired a housekeeper named Vanessa as a gift to Dad. She would come in once a week and clean the place. Despite some initial grumbling, he soon came to look forward to her visits.

Vanessa was scheduled to clean four hours a week. She was really good in the early weeks, but as time went by the kids noticed the quality of her work was starting to slide. Lilly was elected to give Vanessa a "talking to." As it turned out, Dad would engage Vanessa in the kitchen with a couple glasses of lemonade. He would talk her ear off before letting her start working. It put her in a rough position. He wanted to talk; the kids wanted her to clean. She had other appointments on her schedule. Dad was lonely and her boss.

When they had been younger, Mom and Dad had loved to dance. They went dancing once a week. Lilly learned about a group of older retirees that met at the local rec center for dancing every Friday night. Dad was not particularly interested, but Lilly took after her mother. She told him that she would go as his date so he would not have to dance with anyone else, and if he had a miserable time, she would not bring up the subject of dancing again.

It turned out that he loved it. Dad had always been a handsome man and as a result of grieving, he had dropped twenty pounds since Mom's death. He stopped eating out, including fast food, or even going to the grocery store regularly. He ate a lot of PB & J and drank milk. The first time he led Lilly around the floor to the tune of *Satin Doll*, half the ladies in the room were already in love. *What a handsome gentleman! A very good dancer.* Dad breathed in their attention and blew it into his ego like a party balloon. He never asked Lilly to join him again, but he started going every week.

By the end of the first year, Dad was a changed man. He kept off most of the weight. He had more energy, Vanessa was keeping the house clean, and he would even date a few ladies. Most of them were wonderful, and the kids were disappointed each time Dad moved on to someone else. They would joke that it was easier to keep up with him when he stayed at home all the time. His love life was becoming complex.

The kids did not care though. Dad was happy and most of the women were nice. Then, he met Veronica. She wore leopard print tights and flowing purple tunics. She preferred her accessories, especially shoes, to be either gold or silver lamé. Veronica became enough of a fixture in their lives that the kids soon pinned "Lamé" onto her as a permanent nickname. One time Randy slipped and called her "lame" and it stuck. After that they just referred to her as "lame." Veronica was actually very quick witted and had interesting to hilarious comments to make, but the kids really did not want to like her.

The kids wanted Dad to be with a woman who was "presentable." Someone who, though she could never replace Mom, could at least remind them of her, someone who went to church and cooked meals at Thanksgiving and Easter, someone who could be a substitute grandmother and get excited to babysit. That definitely was not Lamé. Lilly was convinced that this was her father's way of getting back at her for dating Nick with his tattoos and motorcycle in college.

Veronica was petite, with blond hair, red lips, big glasses, and two Yorkies named Frank and Ava. She had been divorced for about eight years. She had one son, Jason, who was forty-two and lived in Boston with his family. They did not communicate a lot except when he needed something (which was, in fact, fairly regularly).

Dad thought she was great. After all, he was not looking for a grandmother; Dad was looking for a date. Those other ladies might have been attractive to the kids, which is what made Dad lose interest. Yes, they were wonderful, charming, gracious, warm, intelligent, witty women. But Dad knew their mother in a way they never could, and she was gone. Mom was an impossible act to follow and he was not looking to duplicate what he had with her. Veronica could be funny and obscene, but was seldom vulgar. And well, Veronica did *things*. Aggressively. Veronica had what you might call a healthy geriatric sexuality. To the kids, that sexuality was funny, maybe even pitiful, but to Dad it was hot. In a world of old ladies pretending to be grandmas, here was one woman that wanted to feel sexy and wanted to feel it with him.

Dad had been with Mom most of his adult life. He had not known many other women in all that time, and Veronica's openness to experience was a totally new thing. And as sweet as Mom was, she had had a good number of hang-ups and insecurities. Veronica did not, at least in that area, and she and Dad were having more fun together than the kids could ever have guessed. This is probably why the kids did not have much luck pushing him into the arms of someone they liked.

As their father spent more and more time with Veronica, their relationship continued to blossom. One morning, Dad woke up at Veronica's place after a particularly lovely night. She rolled over, looked him in the eye, and said, *So, are you going to make an honest woman out of me?*

As soon as Dad hesitated, Veronica assumed a look of great sincerity and gravity. Without breaking eye contact, she said, *You need to know that my period is late, and I think I might be pregnant.* Pause. *Well it actually it is about twenty years late.*

It took a long second, but then he laughed the laugh of dumb guy relief, and love and security and friendship. He realized that he was in love with Veronica after that. They did not run off to Vegas right then, but the seed had been planted.

A new guy started coming to the rec center dance about four weeks earlier and was an excellent dancer. He had been a dance teacher as a young man and he swept the ladies around the floor with strength, confidence, and abandon. When he took Veronica out on the floor, Dad got jealous. He even mentioned the situation to Lilly (who was secretly thrilled). She also had to appreciate the fact that she was now seeing her sixty-nine year old father lovesick and jealous. The trouble was that Veronica knew it, too. She was waiting for the perfect opportunity to light a fire under Dad and the new guy provided it.

She had played the carrot and stick routine to perfection. Veronica was very good at giving men what they wanted, but before the new guy showed up, she was not sure what she could use as the stick. She never had any intention of running off with anyone else; Dad was probably the most attractive bachelor at the dance, but when new guy showed up, she laughed and danced and made sure that Dad was watching.

It worked, and after a few weeks of watching this flirtation play out, Dad decided to make Veronica into an honest woman. He told the kids first, but their disappointment was plain to see. He assumed a look of far-away sadness and simply said, *Look guys, she makes me happy. However many years I have left, I would like to spend them with her.* Veronica was not the only one who knew how to manipulate emotions to get what she wanted.

The kids looked at each, thought of their mother's death, and silently conceded his desire to be happy. They actually felt selfish now about their passive-aggressive hostility towards Lamé. Dad had turned the entire family around in under three minutes. It was a thing of manipulative beauty, but with no objective listener there to appreciate it, it went without comment.

A judge married them a few months later. Just the kids and Veronica's son Jason attended.

Over the years, the kids and Veronica developed an unspoken truce and even learned to enjoy each other's company on occasion. Veronica could be very funny, she liked Randy a lot, and enjoyed the grandchildren. Still, everyone, including Veronica, understood that she was not the person the kids would have chosen to be Dad's next wife and would never be. She never lost her love of lamé and leopard skin, but she kept herself in shape and looked great. Above all, she made Dad happy. Because of that, the kids contented themselves to put up with almost anything. There was no babysitting unless Dad was around.

After about six years of marriage and after purchasing both a retirement community home together, a getaway place in Scottsdale, and mingling many of their accounts, they decided to create an estate plan. They hired an old fishing buddy of Dad's, a retired lawyer named Eric. He had prepared Mom and Dad's only other will many years earlier when the kids were little. Those were reciprocal wills. Mom and Dad each left everything to the other, and if both died, then everything to Sam, Lilly and Randy. Before Dad and Veronica got married, Eric advised Dad to get a pre-nuptial agreement to keep his pre-marriage assets protected from divorce and separate for the benefit of the kids when Dad died. Dad and Veronica discussed it but both of them found a pre-nup to be too "unromantic" and both agreed they would always do the "right thing" for the other's family in case anything ever "happened." After Dad and Veronica had gotten married, Eric had advised him to at least try and keep their finances separate. That worked for the first few years. But as they acquired more and more property together, and their finances increasingly commingled, they needed something else. Plus Dad was never very good with money, so first Mom, and then Veronica, took over finances and just gave Dad an allowance. He liked it that way.

Eric drew up new wills for Dad and Veronica, identical in every way. If Dad died first, his estate would pass to Veronica and vice-versa hers to him if she died first. Upon the death of the last of the two to die, his or her estate would be split with one half going to the kids, and the other half going to Veronica's son. So whoever died first or last did not matter. The four kids were taken care of just the same. The wills were a little unfair to the kids since Dad came to the marriage with much more in assets than Veronica and a fifty-fifty split with Jason did not really recognize that disparity. Nevertheless Dad always wanted to act honorably and to be perceived as acting honorably. The honorable path in his estimation was fifty-fifty for the kids and Jason. It was something of a thank you gift from Dad to Veronica. Each of the kids was doing well and while they might appreciate the inheritance, they did not need it. It would be used to put the grandchildren through college. On the other hand, Dad realized that Jason, at any age, would need it for himself. Although each would have recoiled at the thought, Jason and Veronica were too much alike for Jason's own good. Dad got this. The same qualities that made Veronica attractive as an older woman, made Jason irresponsible as a younger man.

The lawyer suggested that Dad do a list of what personal items he would like the kids to have immediately if he died first and that Veronica do the same for Jason. There was no reason to hold on to personal items whose main value was before the two met, especially items belonging to Mom. Dad and Veronica talked about it and agreed that each would keep some sentimental stuff from the other, but at the first death most of a life's worth of clothing, jewelry, early pictures and so on would go to the deceased spouse's family. They further agreed that the last to die would give the remainder to the side of the family to which it really belonged. They decided there was no need for lists. Each would do the right thing if and when the time came.

The time came. Dad died first. He had a stroke ten years later at the age of seventy-nine. Veronica was seventy-three.

ESTATE PLANNING:
DEATH AND PROBATE

Just like divorce, bankruptcy and debt collection, few people go to law school with the goal of doing estate planning and probate. Writing wills and talking about disability and death are not the most exciting things to do with a career. Social crusade lawyers cannot get excited about the prospect of helping retirees sort through their options of not working for twenty years and still having enough left over for "the kids". Money driven lawyers cannot get the lifestyle they aspire to while dealing with typically middle-class concerns; there are only so many billionaire estates to go around after all. So the graduates who choose to do estate planning and probate have a mother or father who was an estate planning lawyer or who use it as a foot in the door of a large firm. Estate planning scores low as an issue of justice, seemingly does not improve the world, is not a license to print money and just requires spending a lot of time listening to people with "first world problems." Lawyers who become estate planners fall into it, usually completely by accident.

But that has not always been the case.

In the 1970s women started getting into in law schools like they never had been able to in the past. The defenses erected by male lawyers and law schools (including state law schools) to keep them out began to come down barricade-by-barricade, law school by law school, and firm by firm over the civil rights years. At first law schools had maximum quotas for women in the freshman class, ten percent, twelve percent, twenty percent as the years went by. But those were gone by the middle of the 1980s. Still those women then had to find jobs.

Like everyone else, eager young women wanted the best jobs out of law school. These have always been the jobs with the biggest law firms in town (or state). What "big" looked like might vary a lot between cities across the country but everyone knew which those firms were. They were located on the right street, at the top of the right buildings, occupying at least one floor if not two or three, and they had lots and lots of lawyers working there, mostly copy and paste clones of each other but nonetheless clones of someone who had "made it." Even if you had no chance of getting a job there, as a young lawyer you certainly knew where "there" was.

Women with the best credentials would indeed get hired at these firms, but there was a catch: women were usually restricted to three areas of practice: divorce, legal research, and estate planning/probate. The medium and big firms wanted to show that they were equal opportunity employers, just not too equal. Firms could not be so equal that women could be allowed to represent a client (and hence the firm) in a trial. There was almost the nineteenth century holdover sense that a "lady" was too sensitive and demure to become aggressive and forceful in court, particularly in front of a male opponent, and of course a male judge.

So firms would only hire a minimum number of women. The biggest cases, especially if they involved court conflicts between businesses, and the highest profiles went to the boy's club as though nothing had happened. Women could either take over all the "dirty" cases like divorce that no one else would touch, or they could be relegated to an office with little or no client contact, cranking out legal briefs, or wills and trusts. In fact, this treatment was one of the reasons that many women went straight to the district attorney's office for a job. Employed there, they could be in court immediately and many went on to become judges.

Emily was a product of that age. Her parents thought that her undergraduate degree in English was perfect for her to be a teacher or even a journalist. When she went on to law school, they wondered why she would want to waste her time in a man's world. Although it did not seem like her, they wondered if her real reason for going was just to find a husband. Her brothers gently made fun of her for wanting to be a lawyer, and between themselves they made bets over how quickly she would crash and burn. They felt deeply threatened and wondered how the dominant family dynamic of beer, bowling and baseball might change if their little sister were suddenly someone with an independent power unrelated to those three pastimes. After all, she was always the one who went crying to their mom whenever the boys used their strength to their advantage. They wondered if she would remember once she became a "professional." In fact, she remembered very well exactly what caused her to go crying to their mom.

While Emily had not forgotten, she restricted herself to gentle digs during family gatherings. She did enjoy holding her status over them. As the years passed, rather than resenting her accomplishments, her brothers learned to like having a lawyer in the family. They liked having a "free" lawyer just a phone call away. Emily liked her brothers coming to her for advice and then thanking her for her help. Like most women in the legal profession, her real problems never came from family resentment, but from the older male lawyers. Their resentment never changed. Most of them were men who had gone to law school on the GI bill after World War II or the Korean War. In their minds, the mere concept of having a woman in a law school class, much less practicing was almost ridiculous or unheard of at best. They acknowledged that a woman might be good at legal research and if she wanted to go to law school just to do that, then so be it. Though they may have had the title of lawyer, they remained glorified legal secretaries paid somewhere between a secretary and a real lawyer. They did not practice law. Those men all knew that women only went to law school to find a husband. And that would be harmless except that there are only so many law school freshman seats and every one a woman with a wedding dress in her eyes claimed, was one less for a man who would have a career in the law, raise a family and be a credit to the practice. So viewed like that, allocating twelve percent of freshman law school seats to husband hunters appeared downright generous.

With real premeditation, Emily was called "babe," "doll" and "sweetie" by her colleagues. Sometimes it was by grandfatherly types who really meant it to be endearing, as though speaking to a granddaughter. But mostly the speakers knew exactly what they were doing. They were not just antagonizing a rival, they were trying to put an uppity woman in her place. Emily received comfort by reminding herself that the generation of men using those so called terms of endearment would die well before her and at some point Mother Nature would re-balance the scales with a new older generation of which Emily would be an active part. Like religion, the law changes one death at a time.

Emily started out in the back room of a big firm, writing appeals. There was not much of the "babe" or "doll" stuff there, nor was there any client contact or room for advancement. She also noticed that Friday afternoon drinks usually took place with the two other female lawyers in the firm and five members of the secretarial staff. Sometimes as she looked around at that group of seven at the bar she would internally scream. By default, most of her friends in the firm were the secretaries and legal assistants. On Friday, the men could wear khakis, but the women were always expected to remain "dressed up." Dressed up meant skirts and dresses and maybe a suit that looked like a man's suit (but don't look like a lesbian).

After five years of playing a part, but never belonging, Emily decided that she would rather be her own boss. She went off with another woman at the firm and started a divorce law firm. If she wanted to be in the active courtroom practice of law, this was the best area for her to go into. And that was when the "honey" and "doll" talk really began. Male opposing counsel used this as a weapon to get to her, to fluster her, to make her angry but not a good anger in support of her client. They sought to generate the anger that would cause her to err, to become overly emotional, and to justify the stereotype they themselves had created. They used it easily and freely while feeling much less restraint than the partners at her old firm who at least realized on some level they were all on the same team and would see each other again the next day. Initially she just vented a quick emotional comeback without giving thought to the response. The men of course turned it around and suggested maybe she was too sensitive, too excitable, too shrill maybe even too hysterical (you know all the terms) to be in the man's world of the practice. As time went on Emily learned to make her response thoughtful and if possible combine a comment that supported her case. The men stopped thinking her overly sensitive and simply started thinking she was a bitch.

The opposing counsel Emily dealt with were all older men who were experienced and personally known by the judges. They laughed easily with each other as part of the fraternity. But after a time, on a very deep level she not only observed that it was not just the clients who became temporarily unhinged during divorce, but that the actual practice of divorce was a magnet for lawyers who were permanently scarred, permanently unhinged themselves. The judges were no exception. She could either continue to work in bedlam or find another area of practice.

It took time to admit it to herself but Emily came to understand in her heart of hearts she was too sane to make a life's work of divorce. After another five years or so she realized the daily combat was neither a statement of who she was nor who she wanted to be. She looked for another way and settled on estate planning and probate. It was a much saner, easier, less confrontational practice, and with a huge client list generated over the course of ten years, she had all the estate planning and probate work she could need. She regularly sent out mailers to old clients, which included a woman named Veronica who had gone through her divorce with Emily as her lawyer some years earlier.

The kids had never seen Dad's Last Will and Testament. They knew he had redone it because he had mentioned it in passing a couple of years ago. That came as no surprise. Of course he would re-write it now that he was with Veronica. The kids assumed that when Dad died his will would allocate a split, perhaps 50/50, between them and her, and that Dad would surely have left them personal items as well. Dad was nothing if not fair, and all the kids were secure in that belief. But Dad was also old school private, so none of the kids would even dream of asking him about the contents of the will.

After Dad died, at the funeral and in the tough weeks that followed, the kids rallied around Veronica and did their best to be a huge support to her. Her son Jason was there as well, but as the kids commented to each other, Jason never seemed to "get it." Somehow the world still revolved around him, and he was good for about two days of sympathy. After that, he returned home to Boston and did not call his mother for a month. As always in her relationship with him, Veronica assumed that she had done something wrong. She started thinking that Jason was punishing her for marrying Dad and bringing in new "kids" when before at least he had been the sole actor in the parent/child relationship. She carried the additional burden of that guilt on top of Dad's death. She never could have imagined that Jason was simply thoughtless, petulant and emotionally ten years old, rather than a justifiably angry adult. When he did finally call, he acted as though nothing had happened. For him, nothing had.

The funeral kept coming back to her: the kids had been so dedicated and kind. But they clearly had held Jason at arms-length, exhibiting no more than a polite interest in including him. Veronica felt as though they were showing off, trying to prove that they were much better children to someone who was not their mother than Jason was to his own mother.

After thinking about it for a while she convinced herself that Jason had not gone home early because of her, it was because of them. How could he compete with that passel of connivers? The realization hit her around 2:00 a.m. about six weeks after Dad died. It brought with it such a relief and lifted such a burden from her. She and Jason were fine; Dad's kids created the distance between them. Jason must have felt so lonely and insecure that he retreated back home. He did not know what to do or how to act. The kids all had each other, but Jason had no one his own age to turn to in this time of crisis. Under that stress it was forgivable that Jason had overlooked the fact that he was now all that Veronica had.

Jason had a relationship with Dad, too. If the kids had not been so selfish, Jason might have stayed longer. That night, Veronica smiled, smoothed her leopard-print nightgown, and got her first good sleep in a while. It would be so good to repair the relationship with Jason. He was the only family she had left. Once that was fixed she moved on to a final thought that maybe she had one more love relationship in her future.

As Veronica realized that the kids were at fault, she wanted to confront them. She wanted the kids to see the damage they had done, but she could not find an opening. Truth be told, the kids had been magnificent in their concern, calls, visits, and even to the point of taking her out for dinner on occasion. Then, as luck would have it, they gave her an opportunity on a golden platter.

Sam, Lilly, and Randy had been discussing the will and had questions about exactly how the division with Veronica would take place. They had heard that there was typically a reading of the will, and they wondered when that would take place, or if it had already. It never crossed their mind to ask a lawyer these questions because it was simply a family issue. They wondered why Veronica had never brought the subject up, but told themselves that she was grieving and that they needed to give her time. They had each heard the horror stories about the surviving second wife keeping everything but they knew that would never involve them for two reasons. First, they were close with Veronica and secondly, and more importantly, Dad would have written his will so that could never happen. They were confident in Dad's love for them. The kids all agreed that nothing should be said about the will or

Dad's estate for a least a month after Dad's death. After six weeks had passed and Veronica had said nothing, they decided that it was time to bring up the subject.

Since Dad's death, one of the kids would stop by Veronica's place in the morning to check in at least once a week, sometimes bringing the chocolate croissants that she loved. Next week was Sam's turn, and all agreed that he would gently broach the subject of the will. Lilly wondered if she should go, but as the oldest, Sam felt it to be his responsibility. He was nervous, and after pleasantries, he just wanted to get it over with and sort of blurted out, *Could I please see a copy of Dad's will?*

Veronica's response stopped him dead. She said the one thing neither he nor his siblings had ever anticipated: *Why?* "Why?" is such an interesting question. Some therapists believe that the "Why" question should never be used because it tends to fail to elicit an honest response. Whenever a person asks, "Why", especially someone in a stronger position, the one asked will always begin to search for an acceptable answer for the asker, rather than the simple truth. He or she mentally begins to search for the correct answer, the answer that the asker may be seeking, to "Why?" At the very least, it causes shock and insecurity in the one asked, especially when unexpected. While no therapist, Veronica instinctively understood all of this. After all, she had landed Dad while operating against much stronger competition.

Sam had honestly expected a simple *Okay, of course,* maybe followed by some sort of apology for not having brought the issue up sooner, along with a sympathetic look of understanding that they both had lost someone dear. Sam had already rehearsed in his mind how he would magnanimously accept her apology and comfort her about her loss; how her mind was absorbed with other things and of course the kids understood that estate issues needed to take a backseat for a while. He had never rehearsed a response to the question of "Why?" The answer to "Why?" must be obvious. It was his father's will. But Veronica just looked at him with a level stern gaze while mentally congratulating herself on pairing the perfect response with the courage to use it. She had no intention of being the first to break the silence. He had to come up with something. She could wait forever. She enjoyed it.

There was no need to wait. Sam promptly stumbled through an answer. *I do not know, just because we would like to know what it says that we get from Dad.* Sam immediately berated himself for using the term "what we get" but on the other hand, while inarticulate perhaps, the statement was the truth.

Veronica said, *We? You have discussed this with the others?* Her voice was chilly, and now Dad's kids were collectively and would forever be "the others" instead of Lilly and Randy.

Yes. Sam was suddenly swimming in deep water with no life preserver.

So all this time that you and the others have been apparently caring for me you've been discussing who was going to get your Dad's money.

Sam went pale. He could not think of what to say. He was not a lawyer or speaker. He just said, *Yes, no, it is not the way you make it sound.*

Veronica just studied Sam for a moment and let a look of hurt and anger cross her face. This was a talent that she had cultivated for years, and Sam was completely flummoxed by it. Sam was always a physical presence and as the oldest child was something of the leader of the kids. Veronica had been worried about confronting him, and could not believe that she had destroyed him in three moves worthy of a Bruce Lee film. Sam was dying to just get out and figure out what to do next. But this was too much fun for Veronica: she was going in for the kill right now before he had the chance to retreat, amend his responses and regroup.

Veronica swelled up with righteous indignation. She had not thought of it in years, but she remembered overhearing Lilly refer to her as "Lame." She had dropped it at the time because she did not want to believe it or cause a confrontation. Even back then she had little communication with Jason and actually wanted to be liked by the kids. But she did notice that the other participants in the conversation did not act like that was the first time they had heard the name.

The way I make it sound? I was your father's wife for ten years! He left everything to me, as a good husband should. There is no need for you to see the will. I can tell you now there is nothing in there for any of you. You and Randy and Lilly are all young and employed with a world of opportunities before you. I'm seventy-three, and all I have is my own small savings and what your father left me to get me through the rest of my life. When that runs out, I assume that I will not be invited to move in with any of you? She thought of that ending at the last moment and just adored the question being like the bullfighting tercio de muerte, the final sword thrust through the heart.

Sam said nothing. He knew she was right, and Veronica would not be welcome to live with any of them. He kept silent partly because he realized that Veronica had been Dad's wife and had made him happy. All of the sudden he felt greedy, and petty, and unsympathetic to an old woman. He realized that Mom if she were alive would be even older than Veronica. He almost told her that she could move in with Jason if need be, but thought better of it.

Veronica just watched at him and waited, enjoying this moment. She had been afraid that she might have to share part of Dad's estate with the kids on some kind of ethical basis. She knew that the kids would eventually bring up the will and she was concerned that Lilly would be the one. Her fear was that Lilly would do it in such a sympathetic, caring manner that Veronica might be placed in a position of having to acquiesce to something monetary, at least as relates to the money Mom left to Dad when Mom died. In that case, Lilly could portray themselves as being as much a victim as Veronica and could make a polite demand for Lilly's mother's assets and it might be a struggle for Veronica to ethically deny that request. Veronica knew that the condo in Scottsdale was purchased largely with Mom's money and life insurance proceeds and Veronica did not want to give up that. So when Randy was the one who made the claim and he did it so clumsily and bluntly, her prayers were answered.

Veronica felt that she was completely ethically correct in keeping everything of Dad's without making excuses, and Randy gave her the opportunity to take the condo as well. She actually resented being placed in the position of giving reasons. Veronica understood human need very well. She understood that the death of Dad was just another crisis that reminded the kids of the death of Mom and the financial and emotional security that life would have continued to bring if Mom had survived Dad. Mom not only was dead, but she had been dead for a long time. Those days were over. On the other hand Veronica was alive and needed security for at least another 15 years. The kids needed to stop whining, stop expecting handouts and live with the new relationship situation into the future just as she had lived with the relationship situation while Dad was alive. That is, just as she had lived with them on the one hand saying, *I love you* to her face and calling her "lame" behind her back. She had sucked it up and lived with it. Now it was their turn.

On a sunny morning with her only expecting croissants and having to tolerate Randy for an hour, the kids had handed her the perfect escape. And she, like the warrior she had always known herself to be, had seized the initiative in the situation and used it to strike a fatal blow. She could be the victim here, keep everything, and even get to enjoy the moral high ground. Who was lame now? Huh? Who was lame now?

But she did not want to leave things in a total mess. Who knows, with Jason now as her main relationship, and no fallback other than the kids, she might have to call on one of the kids for help in the future. Sam was sure to report back to the others and with time to think about it he will certainly have the standard guy response to get mad and inflame the others. It was time for a little kindness. *I do have some of your father's personal items that he would have wanted you, and your brother and sister to have.* She stood up and moved towards the door. *In a few weeks when everything settles down, I'll call you to come and get them.* She almost added that the kids would continue to receive something when she died but thought better of what would clearly be just an outright lie. What she had said a moment earlier was true. Each of the kids was doing fine and needed no outside help. But she, because of age, and Jason because of personality and character due to his worthless father, would always need help.

As Sam stepped into the bright sunlight outside of Veronica's condominium, he squinted and felt the warmth, noticing that the little voice in his mind had gone silent for a moment when he saw the prettiest little purple flower he had ever seen. He walked to his car numb, and arrived home without really knowing how. He knew he had been beaten somehow, but as he mentally glanced back at Veronica; a sad, little old thing with rhinestones in her glasses and a thick layer of makeup, he almost thought that might be okay. Maybe the family was better off without her and the financial loss was worth it. Sam realized one thing with crystal clarity. He could never think of Veronica or refer to her as "lame" again.

For her part, Veronica was elated. She thought about having a drink but decided it was too early. Instead she called Jason. After chastising him for not calling her, he started making noises about work. He wanted off the phone, so she decided to brighten things up.

You are going to have a very nice inheritance from your old Mom.
Jason suddenly was all ears.

The 'kids' have been just horrible and greedy and only coming to see me to sniff around for the money they think they get from the estate. I know the only reason you left so soon after the funeral was the mean way they treated you.

That one went right over Jason's head. He had left for the same reason that he always left: he could only tolerate Veronica in small doses. If anything, Jason had always been a bit embarrassed by how pleasant the kids were to him, especially considering what his mother was like. He reasoned that if he did not want to be around her, he would not blame them for feeling the same way about him. But the words "nice inheritance" sounded good so he said nothing.

Veronica took that silence as an acknowledgement of her suspicions that Jason harbored the same resentments to the kids that she did. She felt, twice in one morning, vindicated and righteous. *You know, their father quite rightly left everything to me. Because those kids are so awfully greedy, I have decided to leave everything to you. After all, you are my flesh and blood, not them. Someday, not today, I will tell you the name they called me behind my back.* Jason mentally went over all of the names he had for Veronica over the years and wondered which one the kids had selected.

Jason did not say shit. He did not want to say anything that might mess with his chance to be financially well off in the future. There was much too much water under the bridge for him to get gushy, lovey with his mom and he did not want to lie. He had always assumed that the kids would receive the bulk of their Dad's estate. Whatever money Veronica had received from her marriage to Jason's father had been mostly spent when she met Dad. Jason had no idea that the new wills gave everything to his mother. In fact, he was shocked that the kids' Dad had abandoned his children like that. Jason had always liked and respected Dad and had wished his own father could have been more like him. The fact that Dad had not given at least some large part directly to the kids at Dad's death puzzled Jason. It made no sense. Jason had expected nothing after Dad's death. It never crossed his mind that he would receive anything from the death of Veronica other than a corpse (as always, with too much makeup), a lot of crappy clothing and an unfunded funeral. His head was suddenly spinning.

Veronica assumed that he was overcome with warm emotion toward her, and if it were even possible, felt even better now about how the day had turned out. In fact, this might have be the best day of her life. She was finally reconnecting with her son.

Jason remained silent on the other end of the line while he mentally estimated how much time she might have left. He had a catalogue of her illnesses. After sixty years of two packs a day, the gods could not delay much longer before inviting her to step into the Void. There was no way she could make it past eighty, seven more years! The only threat to his inheritance was if she wound up needing long-term care. (Veronica sure as hell was not coming to live with him. Jason's wife, Lois, had already made that abundantly clear on repeated occasions). Long-term care can really eat up an estate. He pushed everything out of his mind and decided to think positively about her pending departure. And if she lived too long and spent his inheritance he could get her into a Medicaid nursing home and let the government support her. He came out of his

DAVID M. COOK

reverie and said, *Mom, let's not talk about your death.*

Yes! Veronica thought. *He hasn't called me Mom in forever.*

Sam went home to think. As he relaxed, he mentally played and replayed one of the worst twenty minutes of his life and began to realize what had happened. The last people he wanted to talk to were Lilly and Randy. He needed to save face and maybe even figure a way out of this mess before admitting his humiliation to them. When he arrived home his wife, Jean, asked how it went.

It sucked. He said. He went on, explaining everything and withholding nothing.

Jean listened carefully and said, *It was not your fault. You went to see Veronica with good intentions and she turned everything upside down. There is nothing wrong with a child inquiring about his father's possessions after waiting an appropriate time, which you did.*

So you do not think the problem was that I brought it up too soon and Dad's death was still too sensitive for Veronica?

Veronica has all the sensitivity of an outhouse toilet seat. You could have brought up money a year from today or at his memorial service. It would not have made any difference. She intended to keep everything from the moment Dad wrote the will. On some level, Dad didn't write his will, she did. He just signed it.

Sam began to feel better. *Yeah, that is right! I was the good kid going to see my grieving stepmother and she attacked me! Not the other way around.* Jean always knew what to say.

For her part, Jean knew that she was giving Sam the explanation that he could give to his brother and sister. She could not permit her family to be embarrassed in front of Randy and Lilly. She also knew this family pretty well, and notwithstanding all the ridicule and snide remarks about Veronica, on some very deep, emotional

62

level Veronica was still the Mom replacement. The kids were still looking for someone to be the elder nurturing zone and to tell them that everything was going to be okay, especially during a crisis like this. Not one of the kids would agree that they had this kind of dependency, but it was true. Jean understood that Sam went in with his guard down on some level seeking a communication with a mom, and was totally unable to respond to Veronica's aggression. Jean also understood that Veronica was not a bad person. Had she been, Dad would not have married her and stayed with her. But she also understood that the sickness of greed is strong.

Veronica, on the other hand had no such handicap. It never crossed her mind whether she was a good or bad person. She only scored herself on her successes or failures in getting what she wanted. Since marrying Dad she was doing very well. She knew the score when she saw her old lawyer's flier peeking out from under a sea of paper stuck to the refrigerator announcing that she was now doing estate planning and probate. Veronica was pretty sure that probate meant death law.

Some clients are entirely forgettable. Others remain hauntingly familiar even after years. Veronica was in the latter category. Even though it had been twenty-five years since Emily had seen her, she immediately recognized Veronica. She still wore the rhinestone glasses. And she was always perfectly coordinated – matching gold lamé shoes and purse. Moreover, for 11:00 in the morning, Veronica was wearing an astounding volume of makeup. Emily forced her mouth closed and tried not to stare. And she remembered having the same thought when she had run into Veronica and her new husband at the movies. How did such an elegant looking gentleman end up with her? Worse, of all the possibilities that might have been available to him, how could he have chosen that? If Emily had known he was available she would have introduced him to her own mother. During the years doing divorce, Emily said to herself that while she had an intimate understanding of the path of hostility and revenge, she still could not wrap her mind around the ways of love. Emily's had taken a course in Business Administration. She remembered the precept that sales are not about logic and reason, but rather about the manipulation of emotion. She thought that Veronica would have graduated cum laude.

Emily and Veronica exchanged the usual pleasantries. Emily said that she was sorry for Veronica's loss. Emily had spent a little time going over Veronica's divorce case to refresh prior to this morning's meeting. Veronica, if she remembered correctly, was aggressive and vindictive. She had wanted to "take everything" from her first husband. The two of them had one son, Jason, and Veronica kept affirming that she was not trying to bankrupt Jason's father, but rather just wanted all the assets so she could protect Jason. His father was no good but would easily be able to rebuild his life and probably remarry while she and Jason would be adrift. She had to look out for both of them. Emily thought it was safe to surmise that today's visit would be more about gain than loss. As the reason for Veronica's visit unfolded, Emily smiled to herself. Welcome back to the same old Veronica. Same dance, different tune.

After the polite talk, Veronica went right to the issue. She knew she was "on the clock" and did not want to spend $400.00 an hour to talk social. Veronica wanted to know if the "kids can get anything" from her inheritance. She said it just like that.

After the first blush of victory wore off of her confrontation with Sam, she realized that she did not know for sure if she was on solid legal ground. What if the kids had some right, like she had heard that spouses had, to a percentage of Dad's estate? What if they could file a lawsuit? Veronica had suggested to Dad when they were in the estate planning attorney's office that their wills should contain one of those no contest clauses so if "someone" fought the will they would lose everything. But Dad laughed and asked who in the world would fight it? The wills were fair and the no contest thought went away. Now she really regretted not nagging him until he changed his mind. She knew she could have used Jason as the potential antagonist in her example and Dad might have bought it just to be certain his kids were protected.

And now, what if she had gratuitously alienated Sam, and thereby his brother and sister, when all she had to do was show them the will and give them some of Dad's clothing and the (inexpensive) jewelry and they might have gone away happy. That might have kept her on their good side. If the kids had rights, it was safe to bet that they were already looking for a lawyer of their own. What if she had made a terrible miscalculation? What if? What if? She had been trying to shake all this doubt, but at 3:30 that morning it came back with a vengeance. It would be heartbreaking to be so near, and then to lose it.

Waves of relief flowed over Veronica as Emily explained that only spouses have the right to take assets contrary to the terms of a will, and that Veronica was safe. The fact that the kids were named in the will and actually provided for at the death of the last of the two sealed the deal. The kids were not actually left out, they were just provided for when Veronica "passed" to use the lawyer euphemism for dead. Emily said that last part just for fun to see if she could get a rise out of Veronica. She studied Veronica hard and went silent. She knew that there was no way on God's green earth that Veronica would not re-write her will and remove the kids entirely. Veronica's look was stoic. Her mind was far beyond the will she had made with Dad, which she had already torn up. As soon as

Emily said that the kids had no rights, her mind began to wander.

On consideration, Veronica was pleased, but slightly miffed that the kids had forced her to waste money on this consultation. She wondered if there were some way to make them pay for it. Call it a family consultation to properly manage Dad's estate. For her part, Emily's mind processed on multiple levels: happiness for her client; an almost overwhelming compulsion to stare and just try to comprehend this 73-year-old caricature; and the question of how a family that seemingly got along for over 10 years suddenly devolved into combat over money and possessions.

Emily, over the life of her practice had genuinely tried not to become jaded, especially during the years of practicing divorce law. When she saw that to be impossible, she moved over to estate planning. She understood that she was dealing with humans in times of grief, and that all of them went through the process differently. Emily just wished that clients would stop trying to *make* her jaded. What Veronica's family needed was two hours with a family therapist not legal posturing. But that was not the kind of advice that Emily was being paid to give and Veronica would not have come close to understanding how therapy would help her stay in a nice private pay nursing home when the time came. Plus it looked like everyone was beyond that anyhow. Yes, Veronica told Emily her victimization story. She told her about how manipulative and greedy the kids had been, and the things they used to say about her in the past. And it took all of Emily's self-control not to laugh out loud when she first heard the story of "lame." She wanted to meet the kids. They sounded like fun.

Emily also recognized self-serving bullshit when she saw it, and this consultation had been full of it. Because of client confidentiality Emily could not use Veronica's name when she told this story to her friend at happy hour later that afternoon, even though the friend was also a lawyer. From the moment Veronica reappeared in the office there was never any doubt in Emily's mind that this had all the makings of a two-martini tale. Veronica's fashion taste alone was worth one martini. So normally Emily would just make up a name to insert for Veronica. But after Veronica told Emily the lame reference, Lamé would of course be the alias that she would use this afternoon.

Stifling her impulse to laugh at Veronica's shamelessness, Emily explained that if Dad had really wanted the kids to have anything at his death (even clothing), he needed to either say so in the will or make them the beneficiary on a financial account. The view of the law was that if Dad did not say something, then he did not want the kids to receive anything until Veronica's death. Emily asked if any of their assets were held in joint names. Veronica said, *Yes that our bank accounts were for ease of paying bills and the condo was because when we refinanced the lender insisted that both of us be on the title even though all the equity had been Dad's.*

Well, Emily said, *All of those assets would go to you automatically even if the will had said something different and given part of them to the kids.*

So, regardless of the will, they never had a chance? They both looked at each other in silence for a moment after that remark. Emily wondering if Veronica understood the depth of what she had just said and Veronica reading Emily's countenance and thinking that she was not paying $7.00 a minute for some kind of Sunday school self-righteous judgment of her behavior from someone who, at the end of the day, was just another *fucking lawyer.* Everyone knows about lawyer ethics. At that moment, Veronica vowed to herself that if she ever saw any further moral judgment coming from Emily, she would remind Emily that her entire practice and livelihood were based on human greed and please do not pretend to be superior.

Finally Veronica felt complete. Nothing that had happened was her fault. *That brings up another subject,* she said. *I may want to change the terms of my will and not leave the kids as much. They are all young and productive and married. My son, Jason, has had a tough time and needs more help than the others.*

Emily knew where this was headed, but she had to play along. Both she and Veronica understood perfectly well that Veronica was going to write a new will and leave the kids out completely, probably with one of those no contest clauses, just in case. Emily just had to smile and nod until Veronica built up the courage to actually say so. Emily probably would actually be the one to write the new will; Veronica would be much too embarrassed to recount this story again to a new attorney. And in truth, that was fine with Emily. The two of them had each established a relationship. Although Emily thought, with a little wistfulness, that Veronica was another of those people that made it very difficult for Emily to avoid becoming jaded. And then to counterbalance that emotion, in a flash of empathic insight from somewhere, she also thought, *What a difficult childhood Veronica must have had. You know there was either a manipulative or absent parent, or both, in her history. She did not just become this way all on her on. It must have been kick-started somewhere.*

This made Emily think further. Was it really fair to judge? What was Emily liable to be like at 73? She shook it off. No, Veronica had lied to herself her whole life. The kind of dysfunction on display here was cultivated over a lifetime. Emily gave Veronica her best "is that all?" look, but Veronica was already turning something else over in her mind.

Jason had called her that morning. Like mother, like son, Jason had also been awake at 3:30 a.m. worrying about this new situation. He could not get the question of long-term care out of his mind. He had heard that thousands of dollars a month was not uncommon for a private facility, and he was already pre-spending his inheritance. Since Veronica had put the idea in his head, Jason had started thinking about how much he could use that money. Then he thought about the lifetime he had spent emotionally supporting her and affirming her conduct, when all he ever really wanted was to tell her the truth about herself and never hear from her again. She had always been at a minimum an embarrassment starting with grade school. But now he was suddenly, literally invested in her hopefully quickly diminishing future, and contact from him would need to be more regular, much like regularly reviewing your portfolio to be sure it was safe. It also dawned on him that the money was not so much an inheritance as a well-earned payback for a lifetime as her only child.

After Veronica gave him the news, Jason immediately told the story to his wife. Lois was considerably less conflicted about her feelings toward Veronica: she did not like her at all for what Veronica had done to her husband. Veronica was crude, touchy, and a busybody. And she knew that while as a son, Jason should initiate contact with his mother more often, Lois also knew that such conversations began with polite inquiry into the life of Jason and the family, followed by Veronica's interminable recitation of her problems with an expectation of sincere interest. Veronica had driven off Jason's father and manipulated Jason for years. Lois did not even care about the money - just the fact they were finally going to get something back. As to the kids and their interest, Jason simply assumed that their family had not been as picture-perfect as they let on. Otherwise, their father would have made sure to discuss his will with them and be certain that there was no way that his family could be excluded, even inadvertently, especially after consulting a lawyer. The fact that he had not done so, spoke volumes about his relationship with his children. Maybe he was not the prince everyone thought. Jason felt the need to emotionally tie up this one loose end in his justification why all the inheritance should ultimately be his.

Jason called his mother and explained that a prudent financial course to protect the estate would be to see if Veronica could use a Medicaid nursing home instead of a private one. Jason felt very clever, and phrased it in terms of sound financial planning, asset protection and other terms he had heard from a friend, rather that talking about inheritance. The friend was a high school teacher turned insurance agent, turned financial planner, turned "wealth strategist." Over drinks he explained how Veronica and Jason could "protect" Veronica's estate. Veronica said she would at least think about it. Now that the kids were permanently gone, Veronica felt the need to stay on excellent terms with the only person left to be with her and care for her in her old age. In her heart of hearts she knew that she had to string Jason along on this one. She had worked too hard to get where she was to give it all up, even for Jason. Veronica believed Jason was a good boy and would take care of her, but she really did not like Jason's wife. She could not be trusted, and probably was the one who came up with the nursing home idea as a way to get the money away from Veronica.

About two weeks later, Veronica made an appointment to visit a Medicaid nursing home with Jason. She only lasted twenty-five minutes in Green Valley Senior Living. While on the second floor she smelled urine to the point that she almost gagged. She thought

Yellow Valley would be more accurate. That, coupled with seeing the "seniors" placed like houseplants around an older large-screen TV was horrible. Their bodies were largely un-useable and their faces were forlorn and vacant. This was a place where the living sent the dying in the hopes that they would not have to watch. Veronica excused herself as she headed for the door. Neither she nor Jason ever brought up Medicaid again. Jason could only hope.

The kids were forced to accept the new status quo. Veronica cut off all contact with them and replaced Emily with a different lawyer to arrange her new will. Veronica had not forgotten the look of judgment on Emily's face. She knew that Emily just did not understand that Veronica had simply made her way in a difficult life as best she could and had done a pretty damn good job at it. Lawyers are rich. They do not understand real life in the trenches. It was easy once Veronica realized that since the kids were not blood relatives she did not have to even acknowledge their existence in the new will and so did not have to give a lengthy history to the new lawyer. About a year after Dad died, a box arrived at Sam's house with only a return address, but no name. Inside were a couple pairs of shoes, some clothing, a couple of inexpensive watches, his Rotary Club lifetime member pin and the family photo album from when the kids were young. The kids really were satisfied. The photos helped them realize that no one could ever replace their parents and that, for all the betrayal and disappointment, it had not really been that much about money. About two years after Dad's death, Veronica married a retired personal injury lawyer and moved with him to Boca where her fashion taste fit right in with the locals. Jason just felt more lost than ever.

IT WAS ALL THE FAULT OF
THE CHIROPRACTORS

O nce when I was newly out of law school, I read an advertise-ment for a lawyer who claimed that he was an M.D./J.D. I was as impressed with him as I could be with anyone. I could not imagine anyone going through both medical and law schools. It would be like intentionally repeating Marine Corps boot camp. I showed the ad to another young associate in the firm, Bernie (whose family background included a long line of doctors), and he immediately commented that this poor fellow was a screw-up who could not make it as a doctor. I looked at him in shock as I tried to find the words to defend my new hero. The best I could do was protest that Bernie could not know if the guy went to medical or law school first.

Bernie said, *David, if you had the grades and could be accepted into law school or medical school, which would you choose?"*

I said, *Medical school, of course!* No one makes doctor jokes, but inept me got a 'D' in high school chemistry. The instructor was feeling generous.

Bernie said, *Of course, you're right. Medical school would be the first choice of every other lawyer you know, too. That was the case with your new hero. He went to medical school first, became a doctor, and could not hack it professionally. He had the time, money and grades to go back to law school, and the law schools were thrilled to have an M.D. in their freshman class, unlike a medical school, which could care less about having a lawyer. Hero's medical degree made him perfect for doing personal injury, especially medical malpractice, and he makes as much money as he would have as a doctor and his parents are almost as proud. They never entirely got over their shock from when he said that he wanted to quit medicine. 'But what will we tell our friends?'*

Still, Bernie continued. *He remains a screw-up.* Bernie's heritage of physicians probably made him biased, but it was an interesting new perspective.

B ernie may have been right, but I left the conversation still very impressed with someone who had those two professional degrees. The sense of awe never quite faded. It has been more than thirty years since I had that conversation and the memory of that super-lawyer has never left me. I had never considered it before, but hell yes! I would never have gone to law school if I'd thought I could have been accepted to medical school instead. After all, lawyers like to think that they are the smartest people in whatever room they happen to be. Doctors make them a little less self-important.

It was not always this way, of course. Lawyers and doctors once had a calm respect towards one another. And in truth, doctors represent one of the few professional classes that almost all lawyers respect or at least envy. That is, until the rise of chiropractic medicine and the dreaded Doctor of Chiropractic degree (D.C.). After all, chiropractors have long stood on the fringes of professional medicine. Lawyers began to feel cheated somehow.

It began to feel like there were chiropractors everywhere. And everyone got to use the title "doctor" - that magical title of trust and respect, wealth and service. From the moment a chiropractor received his or her diploma that person was the doctor, and the doctor was always in and was always the doctor. Every reference to the chiropractor in every waking moment was to a doctor. They even will present in writing as Dr. Frederick Jones, D.C. Thank you. Once was enough. I get it. You are a doctor.

Lest anyone conclude I am anti-chiropractor, that could not be further from the truth. On more than one occasion I have hobbled to the office of my chiropractor in debilitating pain and walked out of her office vastly improved and well on the road to healing. No orthopedic M.D. could have done as well as quickly, and without drugs. I am not talking about performance. I am only talking about titles. And titles, as we all have seen, whether Ph.D., J.D., M.D., D.Psych., and so on, while intended to announce years of study to completion in an area, instead can easily become something for the bearer to hide behind. And if many of the bearers in one particular profession use it like that, then intramural competition just about requires that all of them do so.

Lawyers want at least to have the option of a title they could use that way as well, but it feels like all we have to own is a punch line. Every one of us knows the feeling of being introduced and responding to the question, *What do you do?* Then we say, as we study the person's face and body language, *I am a lawyer.* Without fail, the only time we receive an enthusiastic *Oh really, that's great,* response is when a parent of the inquirer was a lawyer. Early on an incipient lawyer did not need a degree to be a lawyer. Historically a person could become a lawyer by going to law school, apprenticing with another lawyer, or simply by taking the bar exam without bothering with either of the first two. In relatively recent times it was not uncommon for a Justice of the Peace to be an elected or appointed position held by a non-lawyer who dispensed simple justice (i.e. pay a fine) in minor cases and traffic offenses. In the twentieth century, if you got pulled over in a small, rural community at 2:00 a.m. and wanted to settle the matter immediately, the police officer got the Justice of the Peace out of bed so he could fine you and send you on your way.

Traditionally a lawyer's first college degree (after undergraduate) was an L.L.B. or Bachelor of Laws. After that came L.L.M., or Master of Laws, and ultimately S.J.D., or Doctor of Juridical Science or Jurisprudence. S.J.D. is a scholarly degree held largely by law school professors. L.L.M. can be a scholarly degree on the road to S.J.D., or in recent years it has also been awarded as a practical advanced degree, such as in tax or urban planning. The L.L.M. is a legitimate and worthwhile course of study for the lawyer seeking to add a title to his specialization but it also appears to be a marketing tool for law schools to reel back in legal graduates to sell one more round of education.

The old legal degree system worked fine. The basic law degree was bachelor's degree followed by master's degree followed by a doctorate. The progression made sense. The Doctor of Chiropractic was a game-changer and created an opportunity for law schools to cash in on the self-importance felt by lawyers.

The D.C. versus mere "legal bachelor" confrontation had to happen because, frankly, cocktail parties were becoming unbearable.

Joe Raferty, L.L.B., had received his legal degree with honors from Stanford. At a Christmas party the hostess, Louelle, introduced Joe to Dr. Williams. They chatted for a while, with Joe taking the lead as he described his position at a well-known downtown law firm. Joe, wishing to make the best impression on this new acquaintance, was careful to address Angus Williams as "Doctor Williams." When Joe's wife, Leslie, stopped by the conversation to say hi, Joe introduced Angus as Dr. Williams.

Joe started to fantasize about bringing the young doctor, who was an enlightened and engaging conversationalist, into his circle. His circle was long on lawyers and shy of any doctors: *Yes, Brittany, I'm playing golf with Dr. Williams this afternoon. Please hold my calls. I will be back tomorrow morning.* It sounded so right, it sounded so good, it sounded so upwardly mobile. Who knows? Maybe someday Joe's daughter will marry Angus' son and Joe could add a doctor to the family.

Anxious for tales of internal medicine, or if luck would have it, plastic surgery, Joe gingerly worked his way into the discussion of Angus' practice. Angus said that he practices with a small group on the corner of 16th and Vine. Joe remembered passing that corner fairly regularly and he had no memory of a medical group. Let's see, there is a Starbucks, an apartment building, an older residence, and the fourth corner is... oh, God, no... a chiropractor's office. The engagement was definitely off.

No need to be polite now. *So, Angus, exactly what kind of medicine do you practice?* Although he knew it was coming, Joe hoped against hope that he would hear at least, family medicine, whatever that means, or even osteopathy. But it was not to be.

Joe looked around, spotted Leslie and waved. He had to go.

In bed that night Joe could not sleep. How in the world does *he* get to call himself a doctor? The small voice in Joe's mind was not objective enough to add, *and not me.* The only reason he went to chiropractic school was that he could not make it into medical school. Leslie elected not to mention to Joe that he went to law school because he could not get into medical school either.

Lying in bed next to Leslie, Joe let an upside-down righteous indignation get the best of him and added, *I cannot believe that Louelle even introduced him as a doctor.*

Leslie, a bit of a social climber herself, responded, *Aren't you overreacting?*

No! What if there had been a real doctor at the party? Someone who actually saves lives, not just tells you that your left leg is a half inch shorter than your right and signs you up for 17 weekly adjustments at $55.00 a pop so you do not walk like Daffy Duck, which you never knew you did to begin with until you went in for your 'free' screening! What if? How would you like to be that doctor and have to listen to Williams get called 'doctor' all night long? It is so ridiculous that even people with a Doctor of Education should be offended! And heaven knows they are the farthest thing from a doctor you can imagine. It makes me want to puke!

What really got Joe the most was not that some imagined surgeon or ER lifesaver might have been offended. The truth was that Joe, with all his background and his Stanford cum laude education, remained a lowly "bachelor" twice over (undergraduate and law). Meanwhile Dr. Williams somehow socially leapfrogged over Joe because he was the "doctor" at the party. You can almost hear Homer Simpson's voice in the role of Joe saying to Marge, *Why does he get to be a doctor and not me?*

The next morning Joe brought the incident up again as Leslie internally rolled her eyes. She was starting to feel a twinge of irritation, too. After all, her mother had told her to marry a doctor, but since she did not like science, she had to do her husband hunting in law school.

Joe did not puke. Instead he traded in his L.L.B. for a Doctor of Laws degree or J.D. Law schools have stopped granting the

L.L.B. and have replaced it with the J.D.: same requirements to graduate, but a new and better title. Never mind that the anomalous progression is now a doctor's degree (J.D.) followed by a regression to master's degree (L.L.M.) followed by a doctor's degree again. Law schools that previously awarded the L.L.B. degree will trade it for a J.D. Literally, just mail in the old degree with a fee and your law school will make you a doctor. It feels like the same acknowledgement that the lion received from the Wizard of Oz. *Congratulations, with this certificate you now have courage.*

The term "doctor" comes from the Latin, and refers to teachers, not to physicians, and thus easily represents the top degree in any field. Joe did not dislike Dr. Williams; he just wanted to get his title, too. Joe is, of course, a caricature, but there is much truth in caricature.

Lawyers will always retain some envy of physicians. They are looked up to, respected and appreciated. Lawyers go into their field expecting to share in some of that, but one saves lives, the other negotiates death benefits. But there is more to it than just that: people automatically respect doctors. Often in estate planning I will go to a hospital or nursing facility to see a client/patient. I always wear a suit and carry a briefcase on these visits. I always thought that I could not have more obviously been a lawyer on these occasions than if I had been wearing a nametag. When I first began doing this, I noticed that people in the hallway looked at me and smiled, and said hello as I passed. I could not quite figure out the smile that was warm to the point of being deferential. Since I assumed that I was so obviously a lawyer, I assumed that everyone who saw me thought that I was sneaking in with a deathbed Last Will and Testament for a wealthy 85 year old designed to take millions from her family and deliver it into the hands of my client, the evil housekeeper.

But just the opposite was happening! Everyone acted very happy to see me, almost deferential. At first I thought maybe people in hospitals were just naturally happier, then I thought maybe it was some quality of my personality that was more pronounced that made people in hospitals feel more at ease. But then why was everyone being so deferential? As it turns out, they all, staff included, thought that I was a doctor, a real doctor.

My heart sank. They did not really know me or like me. They thought I was something that I was not. I did not have to explain that I was not there to maneuver the kids out of the will, because they could never think such negative thoughts about a doctor.

Understand that in my stomping grounds, being in the courthouse was nothing like being in the hospital. In the courthouse, I cannot get anything approaching the treatment doctors receive in hospitals. In the courthouse, the lawyer is a pain, a nuisance, a whiner, or an arrogant asshole. The hospital is just the reverse. In the courthouse it is difficult to find anyone who does not feel superior to the lawyer: certainly the judges do, and even the clerks look upon most lawyers with an elevated disdain. The courthouse is not a home base at all. It is, on the contrary, the scene of battles with all forces aligned against the J.D. unless he or she works for the state.

So at first I was ashamed when I realized why people in hospitals were nice to me. My initial reaction was to avoid eye contact. I felt that I was being dishonest when people smiled at me for the wrong reasons. But they refused to stop. Back at the hospital, older couples would strive to catch my eye, smile and say hello. Sometimes their countenance and body language indicated that they would like to stop me and ask a quick medical question. I returned those smiles with my best imitation of a "late for a big surgery demeanor." They always believed it and did not pursue it. I did not want to have to tell them that I was a not a medical doctor. Although it crossed my mind as a backup defense that I could rehabilitate myself by explaining to them that I was a Doctor of Laws. But I understood that they would be about as impressed with that title as the clerk of the district court.

Nurses, who would not have known that I was a lawyer, acknowledged me in the elevator, even sometimes making conversation. The people were acknowledging, nay, genuflecting to me as a doctor, a real doctor.

So I transformed. If hospital citizens were unwilling to stop treating me like a doctor, then I was going to give them a great bit of half-second surgical charm as we passed. I starting making eye contact, smiling, even helloing them myself while maintaining the bearing of chief of surgery or visiting professor of pediatrics. Truth be told, I even started to resent people, particularly staff, who did not acknowledge me as a real doctor. But I was also cautious not to overplay my hand, fearing that at any moment a perceptive hospital visitor would notice that I was carrying legal papers and might shout, *You are not a real doctor at all! You are just a lawyer!* At that point I would be forced to meekly exit the hospital before the word got out and my housekeeper would wind up penniless and unable to pay my bill.

After a while I tired of my neediness and developed a more reserved smile. I still liked the free greetings, but once secured, I would give my best, "this is just a hello- hello." I had watched real doctors do this many times, so I had it down pretty well. I likened my response to that of a religious leader who waved and blessed and loved everyone from afar, but was cold one-on-one. Honestly, I am not over the thrill yet. After all, I could not get into medical school either, and to this day I love hospital visits when I am dressed correctly. It is the only time that I get to be a real doctor. Well, to avoid feeling guilty I tell myself, *At least you're not a pharmaceutical salesman. You know they dress nice too.*

And all of this began with the chiropractors.

AND PUNISHMENT

Howard Paine was a criminal lawyer. He always laughed to himself about how many lawyers got "side-tracked" or more to the point, never started out on any track at all in the practice of law. People go to law school because their mother, father, grandfather or older sister is a lawyer. Worse, they go because their older sister is doctor and they could not make it into medical school. They go because they have an undergraduate degree in something for which there is no market. Or the degree is in a market that can be painful, like teaching school, and after struggling for a few years they go to law school. Then there is also the small group that went to law school because of their ideals. But whatever the reason, most law students find themselves twenty years into their career and working in fields of law that they never guessed.

Not Howard. He knew exactly why he wanted to be a lawyer. He saw some of the early television lawyer shows. In those days they were all about criminal defense cases. He read books about Clarence Darrow. He knew early on that he wanted to go to court and defend those charged with a crime. He wanted to be a knight, a warrior. He saw himself, sword in hand, defending the helpless and those who could not defend themselves. He saw himself as gallant, brave, selfless, and courageous: a man who fought tirelessly against the tyrannical arm of government and the mob. He knew that tyranny had its roots, not in Washington, D.C., but in the treatment of the average criminal defendant. *How we treat those who have no real way to defend themselves is a mirror of our character*, he often thought. He knew that the great freedoms that we treasure are in large part related to criminal law: trial by jury, the right to confront witnesses, the right to a lawyer, the right to not incriminate oneself, and so on. He welled with pride when he thought of the long line of defense lawyers stretching back through the centuries that constituted his moral lineage. He had now taken his place on the front line of that battle.

Many law school graduates looked forward to court appearances with a certain fear and apprehension. The Navy had helped put Howard through law school and when he graduated, he went straight into military criminal defense. He had loved it. He was thrown right into the courtroom and could not have been happier. Once he had served his enlistment term, he went into private practice with a friend from law school, Frank Worley, who was practicing divorce law. It seemed the perfect fit. Both fellows were constantly doing battle on two fronts. Divorce law and criminal law have much more in common than first meets the eye. Among other aspects, they attract a similar personality of lawyers. For Frank, the first battle was with the other spouse and that person's lawyer; for Howard, the first was with the government and its lawyers. But in each of those two areas, more than other areas of practice, there was also lurking the high potential for battle on another front, with the client. Howard looked upon the wealthier corporate lawyers with disdain. In his mind, the legal field was a lot like the military: law-yers like him served on the front line, they were the line officers. The "line" to Howard was more than just court appearances. The line to Howard was protecting the American justice system and thereby the average person. Howard often would quote Supreme Court Justice William O. Douglas, "The purpose of the Bill of Rights is to keep government off the backs of the people." That is what he did in his own small way. He tried to keep government off the backs of the people.

But Howard had a lot of professional friends from all walks of the legal world. When Howard talked to other lawyers he learned much about the predictable continuum of human personalities. The nature of the client did not really change all that much. After all, when all was said and done, much of what a lawyer had to do was wrangle a client through the legal system. The clients did not always go willingly. Love, fear and greed; take those away and ninety-five percent of all cases go away.

Howard's friend Edmond, a corporate lawyer, complained that his clients were always holding back some piece of damaging infor-mation about their transactions. *Everybody lies, or at least shades the truth, to support their own position, or to show themselves in the best light,* he once commented. *The shading can be very subtle and yet at the same time, it may be very significant. I have to know a business cli-ent for at least six months before I can tell when he is 'shading' or lying.*

That is not a problem for me, said Howard. *After they say 'hello' my clients are always lying. I know exactly where I stand from the start. You corporate types look down on the criminal bar and our clients (un-til yours get caught, that is), but in one sense my clients are much more honest than yours. Their stories are one big 'shade,' to use your term. Your clients are not any more honorable just because they are only part-time prevaricators. I take comfort in knowing where I stand from the start, rather than in the hypocrisy of the business world.*

Edmond did have a comeback, but he could see that Howard had put a little edge on what started as a social conversation and so he let it go. He thought that one thing Howard said was true: the corporate lawyers did look down on the criminal lawyers, almost as much as they looked down on divorce lawyers, and everyone knew it. The corporate guys exuded a certain smugness that might have been a product of a cynicism that Howard could not match. But to the corporate lawyer, the idea that criminal defense lawyers were "knights" or "crusaders," or anyone else with a sword and a principle was nonsense. In truth, so the corporate lawyer believed, a criminal defense lawyer was little more than the legal equivalent of a street cleaner. Howard was angry, though, so Edmond thought better of pointing this out.

Howard understood how someone might feel this way. He had almost laughed out loud when he was at a party and told a stranger what he did for living. The follow-up questions were predictable and got to the heart of the dilemma faced by criminal defense lawyers, *How can you defend someone that you know is guilty?*

Howard would not answer quickly. He would wait, not only for the dramatic pause, but to give others who were close by and listening a chance to feel the full impact.

Ma'am, he would lower his voice and make perfect eye contact, *In my 20 years of practice they were all guilty as hell. In that time I have had maybe three that were actually 'innocent.' The rest were all guilty. I don't defend them just for them. I defend them for you.* The conversation usually ended there because the other person could not figure out what the hell Howard was talking about and just assumed it was more lawyer self-serving crap.

Howard used the term "innocent" even though he should have said "not guilty." It rankled Howard when the evening news would say that some defendant had pleaded innocent.

Innocence, he went on to say, *is a moral judgment between you and God. In the law, people are simply 'not guilty' that is, the state was not capable of proving their guilt beyond a reasonable doubt. Similarly, no one ever pleads 'Innocent.'* He laughed, *I assure you that neither the judge, nor the prosecutor, nor the jurors, nor even you are innocent. The best we can all hope for in this life is to be 'not guilty.' That is why defendants always plead 'not guilty' rather than 'innocent.' That is just the shorthand way of saying to the government, 'I do not think you have enough evidence to convict me beyond a reasonable doubt.' That is what 'not guilty' means. It does not mean I am denying or admitting anything. It certainly does not mean that I am innocent. It is not the defendant's job to prove his innocence. Thank you, Mr. Justice Douglas and the Bill of Rights. In fact, once you convince me I will probably lose at trial, I will urge my client to take a plea bargain and plead 'guilty.' But even then, we do not plead 'wicked' or 'evil.' We do not plead moral judgments. We just plead 'guilty.'*

It is in this interstice that all of Howard's professional life resided. It is in fact why he can defend those whom he believes to be guilty. He is not defending evil, nor proclaiming their innocence, he is simply, defiantly like David against Goliath, standing up against the power of the state. Every day Howard challenged the system to account for itself, to force it to follow its own rules. And in a true Warrior/Hero sense he understood that you don't fight the state because you think you are going to win. You fight the state because it is who you are.

It also rankled Howard that the state called itself "the People." Prosecutorial documents did not say that it was the State of New Mexico versus Carol Cartwright, but rather "the People" or "the People of the State of New Mexico" versus Carol. In Howard's mind, he came a hell of a lot closer to representing the people than any prosecutor did. They represented all that the people need fear. He thought of the ancient Roman legionary motto, SPQR, the Senate and People of Rome. Those are the people that prosecutors represent: the people as embodied by the State, with a capital S. Not the average guy or gal caught in the grinder of a state prosecutorial system pretending to represent some amorphous concept of "the People." Real people had real problems, and the State could never appreciate this. It fell to Howard to hold the line between the individual and that abstraction. "Governments have interests, not morals," is a statement attributed to Cardinal Richelieu. This was another of Howard's favorites since he knew that at the end of the day the government would invariably come down on the side of its interests, not morals.

Rick was a compulsive shoplifter and very good at it. When others walked into a store and saw the detectors you must pass through, the closed-circuit cameras, and the knowledge that the little old lady rummaging around in aisle three is really store security, those slight temptations to pilfer evaporate. But for Rick greater security measures simply upped the ante and made victory all the more sweet. A stolen can of tuna from under the nose of authority was infinitely more fragrant than a purchased New York strip. He enjoyed the thrill of it all. He liked stealing. It was fun and he was a natural talent.

Rick was also a social worker by profession. Originally, he had obtained an undergraduate degree in biology and a job as a high school teacher. He actually enjoyed teaching and building relationships with the students, but realized that his professional fate was probably sealed unless he got a graduate degree. Through teaching, Rick learned that he liked helping people, so he completed a graduate degree in social work rather than biology. Rick graduated with an M.S.W. and a desire to change the world. Unfortunately, the only route open for him to change the world with an M.S.W. was to go to work for the state. Because Rick had gotten along with the school administrators where he taught, he believed that it would be similarly easy for him to get along with the social work bureaucrats as well.

One day in early May Rick was walking through the Lucky Seven grocery store, a small chain in Iowa. All the while wondering why a rural Midwest chain would use a gambling reference in its name (the stores were actually started by seven Viet Nam War Marines who all came back without injury), he spotted roses on sale at $9.95 a dozen. Rick's girlfriend liked surprise roses and he put them in the cart. Only one thing could make it perfect and that would be, of course, candy. He went to the expensive candy boxes. After all, a bag of Snickers would not send the right message. He also thought that $10.95 for twelve ounces of candy was outrageous. He noticed the box was pretty small.

Over the years he had become really good at making mental notes of where security fixtures were placed in any store he entered. A half-bubble mirror that provided a sweeping view of the customers and products monitored the candy aisle in the Lucky Seven. He picked up a box of candy. In one fluid movement, he turned completely around with his back to the bubble, Rick moved as though he had changed his mind and returned the candy to the shelf, but in mid-course tucked it in the inside pocket of his jacket. Rick knew that multiple cameras were under observation by only one or two security people at a time and a quick action could easily be missed. More importantly (Rick had done his homework), he knew that security did not scan for individual acts of stealing but instead looked for customers who appeared to be likely to steal. Rick was excellent at portraying the wandering high school teacher and not the suspicious man in a coat.

Very smooth, very nice, he told himself as he walked away and continued to shop. *Just continue to casually shop like nothing has changed.* The old thrill was back and it felt good. *The nonchalance, the insouciance*, he thought. These characteristics made him popular with his co-workers, his clients, and his girlfriend. Rick thought these were the same characteristics that permitted him to be such a smooth operator in the 'lifting' arena as well. Feeling expansive and even sorry for poor, ignorant Lucky Seven, Rick put a roll of red ribbon in his basket to tie around the candy before heading for the checkout.

He paid $13.76 for the roses and ribbon. The air was crisp with the thrill of catch and the self-aware sense of freedom that always awaited him after a success over electronics. As he headed to his car, he saw a petite red-haired girl in her early twenties walking purposefully towards him out of the corner of his left eye.

He did not get nervous and intentionally moved deliberately until he heard her use the magic word, "Sir." Worse, she kept repeating it: *Sir! Sir, please stop.* Just as "Sir" is used with an unnatural forced respect by the police officer that pulls you over for a traffic offense, the word "Sir" used by the young lady could only mean trouble. Rick realized that while the representatives of the law, be they police or Lucky Seven security, were now uniformly courteous, it did not seem to help soften the threat they represented. It was almost better when they were rude. It was easier to be confrontational when the law started there. Security forces had become more respectful because of public pressure over the years, but they realized that strict courtesy gave them a psychological edge with both the press and the defendant, and in the video of their conduct.

The human mind under stress not only moves with lightning speed but also can engage in amazing levels of multi-task calculation. In a fleeting instant Rick's brain was processing whether he should actually stop or run for it.

This train of thought was momentarily but savagely derailed when he slowed and heard the words of every lifter's nightmares: *Please stop. Would you please come back in the store with me? Please don't make me chase you.*

Options, options, options. Rick was a runner, five miles every other morning. It helped keep him in shape and deal with job stress. Even with their age disparity, he thought he just might make a break for it. She might have the sprint but he had the endurance, and more importantly the motivation. His car might be an issue but he would make up some excuse to get his girlfriend to retrieve it. While the roses and ribbon were in the cart, the candy was still tucked safely in the coat, so he told himself that he already had his thank-you present ready to go. But then he had a sickening realization as he looked down in the flimsy plastic bag that now held the ribbon and roses. He saw the little receipt with his signature sitting loosely on one side. He had paid using his credit card. They had his information on file. *Dumb, dumb, dumb,* he said to himself.

His throat tightened slightly, but he controlled the urge to run.

The thought of the police coming to his house at 5:00 a.m. to arrest him was worse than the thought of facing the music right now. Young Red escorted Rick back into a little office in the rear of the Lucky Seven and asked him about the box of candy in his coat. Rick acted shocked and denied having the candy. He refused to open his coat on constitutional grounds.

Red did not argue. She had pressed a button on her handset that automatically called the police. Rick could have begged for mercy. He could have played up his contrition, returned the candy, and promised never to darken the Lucky Seven's doorstep ever again. He could have done these things, but Rick was caught up in the rush and was not thinking clearly.

As expected, the police were courteous, but with that dark countenance lurking just below the surface. Rick willingly laid the candy on the table before they ever arrived and was effortlessly issued a summons to appear in a month on charges of shoplifting. Rick was embarrassed at admitting he was a state employee but since he made no effort to use his position for gain, the police ignored it. They had seen worse from higher- ranking people than Rick. His girlfriend loved the flowers at least. They made her day.

Rick had a friend, John, who had gotten a DUI a couple of years ago. Rick asked him about the experience and about his lawyer. He told John that he had a friend who needed that kind of lawyer.

John was immediately on to Rick's embarrassment, but said that his lawyer had been okay. *Just another fuckin' lawyer, but he was okay. His name is Howard Paine. Great name for a lawyer, huh? Paine. You are not looking for a friend, though. Did you get yourself a DUI?*

Rick processed. It was certainly possible that through the grapevine John would find out that Rick was seeing Howard for himself. Maybe even just from a chance meeting in which Howard thanked John for the referral. Rick, especially through his social work, had seen too many unimaginable chance meetings like that to believe it could not happen. John, who talked too much anyhow, might even call Howard to see if the referral went through just to enjoy the glow of Howard's gratitude and maybe learn more.

Rick said, *Yeah, too many shots of Jack at a Shotgun's.* Shotgun Willie's was a strip club. Rick thought the story beat too many well whiskies at the Bide A Wee Inn. *You know at closing the cops are waiting to see who comes out of the parking lot. I forgot to use my right turn blinker and they pulled me over. Bad luck after a great night. I got through the alphabet okay, but the Breathalyzer got to me.* Rick's story made him feel macho and he considered getting into physical descriptions of some of the Shotgun girls, but decided to stop. He felt good about owning up to a DUI. It was a good ol' fashioned "guy's" mistake; one that also showed that he was still his own man and not controlled by his girlfriend (especially since everyone believed he was).

Yeah, went to Shotgun's, drank whiskey, and got pulled over. Well, fuck it.

It was an infinitely better crime than shoplifting chocolate candy and getting caught by a seventeen year-old girl. A DUI is almost a rite of passage, a badge of honor. Getting busted for jacking candy was like having a huge "L" branded on your forehead for "Loser," or worse, a stupid wussy who got caught by a kid young enough to be his daughter. There was no good spin to put on this situation; it was humiliating. Rick started to mentally play the "what are you in for?" conversation that he might have to have in prison, but forced his mind not to go there. No chance he was going to jail. He had priors, but those were long ago and far away.

*H*ello, Mr. Paine's office, this is Viola.
     My name is Rick Slidell, I am a new client.
Is this regarding a criminal case?

Yes. Rick internally recoiled and got nauseous at the use of that term. He was not a criminal he just made a mistake. Criminals use guns and rob people, not just grab chocolate, for God's sake.

Rick got an appointment for two days hence. Howard and Frank's offices were, like all good criminal and divorce lawyers, close to the courthouse. Once contemporary, the offices were slowly showing signs of age, not shabby, just getting worn. In fact when Paine and Worley moved in to the offices eighteen years earlier all the furnishings were purchased new. But a lot of guilty and despondent people had come through over the years, and everything, including Paine and Worley, was starting to show signs of hard use and neglect. Additionally, furniture was expensive and that impacted the firm's bottom line. Unlike at Edmond's, the corporate lawyer's place, there was no need to impress with the office. Impressions took place in the courtroom.

It was not that the green plants were fake that bothered Rick, but while he never thought of himself as prissy, he could not help but wonder why no one seemed to have dusted them in a long time. How could the middle-aged receptionist not notice? She basically looked right at them from her vantage behind the counter all day long. *If the plants were in her home, I bet she would notice,* thought Rick.

Wait. Rick looked again.

The receptionist did not just sit behind a counter; she sat behind a large, seemingly bulletproof, Plexiglas window. Those on the wrong side, on a number of levels, communicated with her by speaking through a small metal vent. Papers could be slid through an opening at the bottom.

Wow, Rick mumbled to himself, *What are they afraid of?"*

In many respects the office was simply an honest reflection of Howard's state of mind. It was still functional. The chairs worked, the couch worked, the magazines worked, the lights worked, the dusty plant worked, even the receptionist, Viola, worked. It all worked. Any money on furnishings reduced profit. Criminal clients came to Howard because they were desperate, not because they were loaded. This was not a foo-foo corporate law office where the client needed to smell the old leather, see the modern Italian lamps, and the pretty young blonde receptionist who immediately solicits your refreshment order. Criminal clients, except the highest white-collar players, wanted emotional, not creature, comfort.

No matter how desperate a person is in divorce or bankruptcy or business, there is no negatively motivating thrill like the black hole of the lockup: gangs (invariably not your race and immediately resenting you), drugs as fun, sex as punishment, homemade shives, the heat, the smell, the lack of air and sunlight, the wretched food, and the noise - no one ever thinks about the constant background and foreground din of noise. But perhaps the worst part was the knowledge that no help would ever be coming. The guards were not there to help. Your fellow prisoners certainly were not. And the outside world considered the convict beyond the pale. If a person on the street were in need, the attitude of most of the public would be to assist. But once in lockup, the public's attitude was best expressed through *Law and Order* clichés:

You made your bed, now lie in it.
You should have thought of this before you committed the crime.
Don't do the crime if you can't do the time.
You are getting what you justly deserve.
What about the victim?

For every crime for which you got caught, you probably did ten
  unnoticed.
Decent citizens are better off with you off the streets.
Maybe you will learn next time.
Stop whining.
You will be a lesson to others.

The last one often made Howard think about how the law is applied. Judges and prosecutors sometimes justify harsh sentencing as an example to others. But nowhere in the statutes is making an example of someone ever mentioned. Punishment should be for that individual alone, and not to pretend that whole classes of similar individuals are also in the courtroom. Howard smirked a little more and then wondered how much a deterrent setting an example really was. It certainly never seemed to diminish his business one bit.

Howard sometimes pondered what it must be like to face prison. He knew that the prospect haunted his clients day and night. Howard had been in prisons as a visitor many times. But when the steel door closed behind him, even for the hundredth time, and even knowing he could always demand to leave, a small part of him wanted to start screaming to be let out. How could one endure years behind bars? It was one of the qualities that made Howard a fine defense lawyer. He got to know these people as people, and finding one who really deserved to be wholly severed from the community was hard - even for him. He frequently said to himself that he must push and strive to do his very best because, regardless of whatever difficulties or hardships that he might face working a case, they paled when compared to the real dangers faced by his clients.

Rick filled out the paperwork on the clipboard with the pen pushed at him by Viola through the slot at the bottom of the window. He left the space blank where it asked about prior convictions and slid it back to her. Viola had something of a grandmotherly look and dress about her. It was not until the second deeper glance that Rick noticed the hardness there. There were no smiles hidden behind her eyes. Rick made a pleasantry that Viola ignored. She heard him just fine, but liked to pretend that the window made it difficult. Viola was not mean. She simply, like everyone else, subscribed to several of the ten premises stated above. Also, she well knew from Howard and from reading his clients' files that they were all guilty as hell of something. Viola lived alone. Her one daughter lived a thousand miles away. The men who saw her grandmotherly look and hoped for some sympathy did not understand that at night, they were the very same men that Viola feared. She did not feel compelled to lie and give them a fake smile.

For Rick, the hardness in Viola's eyes was something that he would get used to over the next few months. The deputies, the court clerks, the prosecutors, heck everyone, would give Rick, as the defendant, that same hard, vacant, look. Everyone who encountered his case had made up his or her mind already. Rick was no longer among the good people. He was outside. A criminal.

Viola buzzed him in, and Rick entered the first office on his left to meet Howard. Howard only looked up from reading Rick's clipboard and motioned him to sit. No handshake, no smile, just sit, stay. Howard's office was borderline shabby and disheveled like the waiting room. He had his degrees, license, and a picture of himself in Naval dress uniform on the wall covered, like the plants, in a thin layer of dust. The walls were of that wood paneling so popular at one time, but now they just looked gloomy and dated. The windows had venetian blinds partially open to cloudy and smudged windows.

Do you have any prior convictions? asked Howard.

Yes, but just shoplifting.

How did you get your job with the state with those?

They were in another state and both were about 10 years ago. The records check did not turn them up.

So you lied to the state about your past?

No, well yes, I guess. Not even a minute in and already Howard was calling him a liar.

What were the convictions?

Both for shoplifting.

Okay. We do not know, but the prosecutor may well have records of those convictions, but if they were at least ten years old and in another state we should be okay. We can probably get you off with a fine, unless you have some defense I do not know about.

Rick felt buoyed by that. It seemed that life would be okay after all. He asked if his employer had to find out.

Only if you tell them. Give Viola a check or credit card for $2,000.00 on your way out and I will see you at your first appearance in court. Annoyed but without better recourse, Rick thought that $2,000.00 was a lot of money for chocolate.

Howard did not feel buoyed. Howard went mentally back to his rule about lying. Rick presented well, but if he had lied about those convictions, if there were more, or if they were more recent than he claimed, it would be trouble. Howard was not really bothered by Rick's past or even his crimes. Howard could care less about that. After all, right now he was defending a man who murdered his wife and then buried the body, as well as two first-degree sexual assault clients. Rick was a minor criminal and hardly worth getting too upset about. But Howard would be unhappy if Rick's faulty memory embarrassed Howard in front of the prosecutor.

Howard had spent plenty of time in the court that would hear Rick's case. The prosecutors were all young, tasked with handling minor offenses such as Rick's. So Howard was very surprised when he saw that Rick's prosecutor was normally one who handled serious crimes. Worse, it was the same lawyer that Howard had recently defeated in a case in which he should have lost and she, Danielle, should have won. Losing is particularly hard on prosecutors because they do not expect to lose, unlike defense lawyers who know losing is a constant, or at least highly probable professional risk. Prosecutors can recite their "win" percentage, normally above the 90th percentile. For defense lawyers, it would be too depressing. Prosecutors hold another ace as well: they can choose to try only cases where they feel assured of winning and can offer enticing settlements in cases that feel iffy. The likelihood of the defense settling is enhanced if the prosecution charges the defendant with multiple crimes stemming out of the same incident. Howard observed in the years of his practice that prosecutors loved to pile it on when it came to charging. He thought charging crimes was becoming like creative writing for prosecutors. Under Howard's noble outlook on his work, he believed that a prosecutor's primary goal should be seeing that justice is done, not maximizing jail cell occupancy rates. But Howard was honest with his self and knew that dream had nothing to do with reality. Chief prosecutors don't get promoted to mayor or to a big law firm over social welfare issues. They get promoted for convictions.

Heavy-handed charging is a practical way to force defendants to plead guilty to a crime whether they believe that they are guilty or not. It is also a way for the prosecutor to look almost benevolent by dropping four charges if the defendant will plead guilty to one, all the while knowing that the sentencing outcome would probably be the same no matter how many charges ended in conviction.

And this process can get ugly. Even if a defendant is convinced of his innocence (or his not-guiltiness), or at least is convinced that the evidence against him is insufficient, his lawyer reminds him that jurors believe things like:

The police do not arrest innocent people.

Even if they do, the prosecutors do not prosecute innocent people.

Where there is smoke, there is fire.

You are probably guilty of something or you would not be here.

You will enter the courtroom as a presumed criminal (possibly in an orange jumpsuit) regardless of the contrary presumption.

And do not pull the excuse that you had an unhappy childhood; so did I and I'm no thief.

Depending on his or her own confidence, the defense lawyer will sometimes point out to the defendant that there is a fifty-fifty chance of conviction even if you are innocent or the evidence is weak. And conviction may mean prison while the offered plea agreement may not. The client will usually succumb to the temptation of normalcy and freedom, and agree that he is better off guilty even with a criminal record. The deal is no respecter of the truth.

Losing for the prosecutor is humiliating. A loss only shows that the prosecutor did not know when to prosecute or just offer a plea deal or even dismiss the case. Howard beat Danielle in a case he should have lost and Danielle knew it. Incidentally, whether Howard's client was guilty or not was beside the point. As Howard said, *They're all guilty as hell.* Once in a while a jury will send a message or set an example as well. In Howard's win the jury actively did not like or entirely believe the arresting officer. Danielle needed vindication against Howard, and Rick's case was the perfect opportunity. Howard understood all of this as he shook Danielle's hand later that month. They both did.

I am prosecuting your boy as a habitual offender. He can plead guilty to this last offense and do the maximum one-year in the county jail. If we go to trial I am asking for the full seven years. Danielle's face did not smile, but her eyes did.

Damn. She probably knew something that he did not. Howard heard himself say, *Rick says that he only has two priors and both at least 10 years ago.*

Your boy, Danielle said (she loved talking about defendants to their lawyer this way), *has been arrested five times as an adult for shoplifting and pled guilty three times. One was fifteen years ago, one nine years ago, and one seven years ago. I'm betting he's a habitual thief who had a lucky streak until this one.*

Howard immediately picked up on the "as an adult" phrase and very much did not want to ask, but he knew must. *Juvie record?*

Three arrests and three convictions. And by the way, in the state where he grew up you are not an adult until age twenty-one. His last conviction was at age twenty, which would have gone on his adult record here.

Howard sighed. He would speak to Rick and get back to Danielle. Danielle left feeling buoyed and could not wait to get back to her office and tell everyone, especially her boss, about the look on Mr. Hot Shot's face when she played the habitual offender card. It had been priceless!

Howard left feeling mad. He took pride in doing his job well, and Rick had not just told him a little white lie. He had left Howard looking completely unprepared to work the case. On the drive back to the office, his mind played through all of the things he wanted to share with Rick: *The miserable lying little shithead social worker prick. Well, I hope the stupid fuck likes boys. Mr. Rick you are about to get all the sex and drugs you can handle. Enjoy.*

R ick got buzzed through to see Howard the next day. Rick had been up all night. He did not know the details, but he knew that Howard's meeting with the prosecutor had not gone well.

We have a problem, said Howard as Rick came in. Of course, what he wanted to say was, *You're fucked.*

Howard explained the habitual criminal statute and how the prosecutor can use it even in cases of non-violent crimes where a person has three or more offenses in the last ten years. This current offense counts as one of the three. Howard always took the position that his job was to make the future better and not level recriminations, but he could not help but bring up their earlier conversation about prior convictions.

Rick just looked at the floor and said, *But I'm not really a criminal. You know.*

Howard nodded. Professional conduct prevented him from staring, open-mouthed and dumbfounded at his client's singular refusal to take some measure of responsibility. After all, he was a fucking thief! And employed by the state for God's sake. He was also a moron who got caught stealing a box of candy. This whole thing might have gone away if he had humbly apologized, paid the money, and promised to never enter the Lucky Seven again. Worse, having Rick's list of priors going back to the age of fourteen was not going to do much to get lighter treatment. At least one bright ray of light for Howard was that he was going to make a lot more than $2,000.00 off this case. Rick was going to pay for his transgressions and paying was going to begin at Paine and Worley's.

Howard snapped out of his reverie, which Rick had misinterpreted as a moment of thoughtful reflection. Finally, he said, *Yes, I know you are not a criminal like on TV, but in the eyes of the law you are a career shoplifter. Career does not mean that this is how you make your living, but it means that it is a way of life.*

Rick thought for a moment. *What are our options? She cannot really be serious about trying to put me away for seven years over a ten-dollar box of candy, can she? I mean, she must know that we will try it and appeal it if necessary, and why would she spend all that time and money from her office over such a minor offense or even series of offenses? There was never a gun. No one got hurt. I promise I have learned my lesson and I will never shoplift again. It feels like she has singled me out but I can't figure out why.*

Howard raised an eyebrow at this. Overcoming the urge to say, *Wanna bet?* Howard went into distracted thought again and pondered his moral dilemma. It was not fair to say that Danielle was enervated over treating Rick as a habitual criminal just because Howard had won the Ross case six weeks earlier. She would never admit that. Howard knew Danielle to be a fine, honorable prosecutor. When she decided to quit the District Attorney's office and double her income, Howard would be glad to take her on as a junior partner. The habitual criminal statutes were, under the laws of the state, perfectly justifiable in this case. To imply otherwise would be unfair to Danielle. However, it did feel a little like she was exhibiting a perceptible, but not quantifiable, level of enthusiasm for the charge that had some nexus to the Ross case. If the charge were both legal and in Danielle's discretion (which it was), and her mind was split as to whether she should bring the charge or not, the Ross case might be the thing that pushed her over the edge.

Of course, he could not say any of this. Howard knew if he articulated that thought to Rick, then Rick would in all likelihood simply fire him and try to find someone more on Danielle's good side to negotiate his case. This probably would not work though. First, it was already too late because Danielle had already played her hand. She could not retreat even if her own mother was negotiating for Rick. Worse, she probably bragged already to her colleagues back at the office, and that made it doubly hard to back down. Second, if Rick fired Howard, then everyone in the DA's office would know why it was done. From their perspective, Howard would have lost this one before he ever even got in the ring to fight. Howard did not like that. He prided himself on his reputation with the DA's office; that he could be tough, that he was a skilled trial lawyer who was not afraid to take cases to trial, and that he could win the iffy ones. He could not, particularly at this stage of his life and career, let that happen. Further Rick might decide there is a legal ethics bar complaint against Howard and ask for his $2,000.00 back.

So, he chose not to tell Rick about the Ross case or his thoughts about one of the items that might be motivating Danielle. *What the hell*, he thought, *what's done is done.* He could not ever really know whether she would have decided to charge Rick as a habitual offender if someone else was the defense counsel. What's happened here was not his fault. It was more properly Rick's. If Howard had known everything from day one, he never would have taken the case. Now it was too late, and the best chance everyone had was to play the hand they had been dealt.

But justifications were just that, and in the back of Howard's mind the voice that drove him into criminal defense reminded him that while he might be embarrassed by the outcome, Rick's entire life was on the line. Rick risked a lot: a minimum of a year in prison, his job, his relationships and likely his home. Rick was not a tough guy or a thug. He was in fact not a criminal "like that" and he was not the kind of person who would survive well behind bars. *He's just a fucking social worker.*

Danielle has offered a year in the county jail as a plea agreement, but I think I could get her down to six months with work release. That means during the week you can be gone from 8:00 a.m. to 6:00 p.m. to work, but weekends you remain in jail. That 8 to 6 window includes travel time, and if you come back late without a really, really good excuse, they will terminate the deal.

Rick had already stopped listening by the time Howard got to the description of a work release program. His mind went blank at the words "county jail". After his first offense at age 14, the judge had ordered Rick to participate in a "scared straight" program at the local jail. It gave him nightmares for years and made him decide that, whatever else happened, he never would go there. It was one of the main reasons that he did not shoplift again until on a dare at age 17. He managed to get away with it then, and gave himself a renewed addiction to the rush.

Rick looked down and just said, *I can't go to jail. Is there any other way?*

No. Danielle believes that you have skated too long. Honestly, Rick you do have multiple arrests and but for a few hours in a holding cell once, you've never done any time. No matter what, she wants to see you in jail.

Rick had to admit that as a young person the courts had cut him a lot of slack, believing his was a case of boys just being boys. Back in those days businesses did not push for prosecution like they did today either. Time had made the system more vindictive than it had once been. As for his later offenses, he just had easy prosecutors who were willing or lazy enough to let it go with a fine and threat. It all made Rick wonder why Danielle seemed to have it in for him, but he had not a clue.

Work release did not sound much better. Rick looked forlornly at Howard and said, *You know there will be nothing to release me for, because I will lose my job.*

Howard nodded. He knew that. Rick was a state employee and the state took a dim view of convicts on the payroll. But it was also the case that people would do anything to get out of jail for fifty hours a week. Even if it meant working at the Gas 'n Go for minimum wage, it still beat the cell. Howard decided to hold on to this perspective. Rick did not look ready for that yet.

Well, what if we try the case? asked Rick.

What case? You have no case. You were caught and you admitted the crime.

But what if we can get a shrink to say that I have a disease and I'm compelled to shoplift and I can't help myself? Something like temporary insanity? You know, it is really kind of true, I can't. It felt better to flip sides and be the victim rather than the Lucky Seven. After all, Rick did not really believe that he was a bad guy. He did not feel "guilty." He looked at Howard hopefully, and smiled for the first time since the meeting began.

For his part, Howard could not believe he was actually hearing this crap. His mind lurched: *you fucking idiot, every criminal wants to think he is not responsible for what he did once he gets caught. You're not sick you're just weak. I do not do the Twinkie defense.*

Howard knew how to get Rick to be sensible. He said, *If you want to try this case it is going to be a minimum of $20,000.00 plus costs, probably another $10,000.00 for your shrink and other experts. I will need $10,000.00 up front and a mortgage on your home to secure the balance. And honestly, I think you are going to lose even if you do all of that.*

The smile faded. Rick said he would go home and think it over. Howard said great, and added that since the case had now taken a new and confrontational, twist that Rick needed to leave another $2,000.00 with Viola on his way out.

She gave him a rare smile as she took the check.

Rick went home. Each evening after work he normally smoked two joints to relax. His connection was the wife of a deputy sheriff who lived one floor below. The deputy usually kept some product from drug busts for his wife to sell to her friends, a nice stay-at-home job for her. Tonight Rick took a Vicodin that he had gotten from one of his clients along with the marijuana, but it did not make him feel better, just sleepy. As he dozed off in his chair he tried to think of ways to rat out the deputy and his wife in order to make some exchange instead of going to jail. But he just could not figure out how his admitting to drug use as well as to shoplifting was really going to help his case. This had turned into a very emotionally expensive box of candy.

Howard had a problem. The problem was not just Rick. On any given day, Howard had over fifty open active criminal cases ranging from DUIs to serious felonies. He even had a death penalty case going to trial in three months and should really be focusing much of his thought on that. In the grand scheme of Howard's workload, Rick was just a minor detail. But there was something else going on. He knew it, Danielle knew it, Danielle's boss, District Attorney Edgar Jameson probably knew it, and hell, Viola probably had gotten a whiff of something that made Rick's case special. Howard slept on it.

At 4:30 a.m., his eyes flew open and Howard knew what it was. Rick's case *was* important. In fact, because of Rick, Howard was engaged in a battle for his very soul and the souls of all criminal defense attorneys. If his winning a case like the Ross case carried the risk of repercussions from the DA's office, then the very heart of his profession was at risk. He needed to know that by doing his job well, he was not endangering future clients like Rick. Of course, Danielle had every right to play the habitual criminal card. She had every right to come at every case with the maximum force available to her. But maybe because of the "tough loss girlfriend" remark he made to her after the jury verdict was read in the Ross case, Howard was being taught a lesson. In Howard's mind, he had not been out of line when he made remarks like that to opposing counsel. It was his way of psyching them out. Regardless, his issues should not burden his clients. By 5:00 a.m. Howard had resolved that the Rick case was a "moral quest." In a moment of early morning excitement, Rick's case had taken on religious dimensions. He was going to go and see Edgar Jameson.

Edgar and Howard had been good friends in law school. Both of them were idealists and crusaders who saw the law as a means to do good for society. Edgar had even tried to bring Howard on board the DA's office, but Howard could not do it. Howard did not come from wealth. His family had been of simple means and devout faith. A lot of his friends had been criminal defendants themselves. Had it not been for the character and strength of his mother, who knew how Howard's life might have proceeded? All these years later, that faith and his mother's lessons still influenced Howard. In moments of severe crisis, such as whether to join the DA's office, Howard would imagine himself, standing at the pearly gates defending himself to Saint Peter.

He would locate Howard's name in his book and begin his

questions: *I see that you had great parents, great brothers and sisters, and you graduated from law school. What did you do with your law school degree?*

Howard would then think back over his many successful years as a prosecutor and say, *I did my best to lock people in cages.*

St. Peter would then push his glasses up on his nose. *Say what?*

Just criminals. Howard thought the reply sounded a little weak.

How did you determine which of my children deserved to be caged?

The question would make Howard's spirit sink a little and he stumbled to answer. *Well, you know, if I thought they had broken the state laws.*

What state?

Howard was not sure if his spirit could feel nausea in the great hereafter, but in his fantasy, it always did. *You know, Colorado.*

I see that you were devoutly religious and learned, and you have read the admonition not to judge. As you stand here now, free of the laws of men, free of the pressures of your culture, free from what St. Paul called 'principalities' and what you call 'the State of Colorado,' do you believe that you made the highest possible use of the gifts given you?

After that, Howard could only humbly apologize to a fairly stern looking St. Peter, which left Howard wishing he could re-live his life. It was enough to make Howard stand on principle, even when it might be easier not to do so.

Edgar agreed to see Howard without any trouble. In addition to their history at law school, Howard once held a fundraiser for Edgar as he was campaigning for a second term as DA. Edgar had heard about Rick's case, and guessed that was the reason for the visit now. They set up an appointment that same week.

After exchanging the usual pleasantries about family and work,

Howard said, *You know why I'm here, right?*

I do. And you know I cannot and will not override Danielle. She is a fine assistant DA doing a fine job. Between you and me, and just between you and me, she may well be the next District Attorney. Besides Howie, your boy deserves a shock. A year with the guys in cell block D will help him rethink his ways. You know he has had plenty of chances. He might not deserve seven years, but that is not really what we are talking about. Admit it. He is a habitual thief and he is not going to change until he sees how bad it can get. Plus he is not really looking at seven years, just one.

Howard had heard all of this before. The truth was that a guy like Rick was going to change in prison, but certainly not for the better. After a year with the guys in cell block D, and all the sex crimes and tainted drugs he could handle, not to mention the latest shoplifting techniques he could get from real pros, the broken, dangerous man that would walk out of there would not be the same one that walked in. The high school teacher and social worker will be dead and buried. Given the choice, it might almost be better to give him the seven years.

But Howard also had no idea how to reform Rick and knew that all of Edgar's points were dead on. This was a lot more than road rage driving school could cure. But the beauty of being defense counsel was that none of that mattered. His job was not to protect society. His job was to get Rick the best deal he could. There were bleeding hearts on both sides of the questions that could worry about our poor society or our poor Rick. Howard did not need Edgar's sympathy, he needed his cooperation so that the case could be handled and everyone could move on.

Howard rubbed his chin as he thought things through. *Okay then. What can we do?*

Like I said, I will not tell Danielle to do anything on this, but we are having lunch later today. I will let her know that, if it were me, I would be okay with nine months and a work release at the Gas 'n Go. I assume they will soon shit-can his ass at Social Services if they have not done so already.

Come on Ed. You know your jails are overcrowded. It was in the headlines two mornings ago. Whatever lesson he is going to learn he can learn in six months.

Edgar frowned and said, *I'll think about it.*

That is all I can ask. Say hi to Jeannette.

You bet. And hi to Louise.

E dgar was true to his word. His lunch with Danielle took place at the cafeteria in the courthouse. Their conversation looked serious and important. But then, so did everyone else's. Not a lot of smiling or joking went on in courthouse cafeterias. After covering a few other points of business, Edgar asked about Rick's case.

I wondered when you would get around to this, Danielle said. *You are not going to twist my arm or give me an order are you?*

Nope.

That almost worried Danielle more. Edgar was being really cool, so he must want something pretty badly. When Edgar had a goal, he got quiet, not demanding. It is how he could produce the image of a calm, seasoned office head that never exploded or got too demanding while getting exactly what he wanted from the people who worked for him.

The little shit deserves seven. An offer of one year is downright generous. We both know that he has stolen twenty times for every time that he's been caught.

Edgar nodded. *I know.*

Then why bring it up?

Everyone knows you got stung pretty bad in the Ross case. Do not get upset, I am one of your biggest supporters. And when you move up to a higher office, I'll be the first one in line to recommend you. It is just that it kind of looks like you're coming down on Rick because you are upset with Howard. Six months will send the same message as twelve and, hey, if you read the newspapers, you know the jail is getting really overcrowded.

Danielle wondered why men always use the word "upset" exclusively when referring to women. Edgar would never accuse a male colleague of being upset. But this was the first time that Edgar had alluded to her replacing him when he moved on. Edgar had a lot of political pull and almost everyone believed that he was going places. His support would be crucial if she were to be the next DA. Then she could tell the guys not to get upset.

Her face was a mask when she said, *I'll think about it.*

That is all I can ask.

Rick pleaded guilty and got six months in the county jail and a work release at the Gas 'n Go. At sentencing the judge told him that he would probably be charged as a habitual offender the next time. Rick nodded, holding back tears, and internally vowed never to shoplift again. He would in fact break that vow within three weeks of release. He went back to a different Lucky Seven (can't risk the red head) and stole six Gillette Fusion razors using a sleeve technique he learned in jail. It felt like justice; as a convicted criminal, his degree in social work was fairly useless. Now he stole in order to supplement his income at the Gas 'n Go. His thrill-seeking hobby became a part-time business.

Edgar became a circuit judge, but eventually longed for his old position as DA. As DA he had been in charge. Now he was just one of many judges putting in ungodly hours. His fellow lawyers might have been jealous or even looked up to him in his new role, but it was a lot more work and a lot less power. Even as DA he had never succumbed to the myth of self-importance, so a large part of the allure of sitting on the bench was missing for him. He talked to his wife about quitting, but she and the kids loved the prestige of him being a judge, not just a lawyer. They would have none of it. His wife told him that she had put up with too many campaigns and too many cocktail parties with people she hated for him to quit on her now. He dropped the subject and started counting down the years he had until he could take an early retirement.

He also betrayed Danielle and did not support her in her bid for DA. As it turned out, a condition of his judgeship required that he support another person for the DA. Fortunately, that person lost the election and Edgar did not have to feel as bad about leaving her in the lurch. He told himself that she would have lost anyhow that year, and he had kind of saved her the pain.

Danielle eventually went to work for Howard, and in no time was making twice as much as Edgar the judge. This gave her an enormous sense of satisfaction, almost as much as Edgar's discomfort when she appeared in his court. Edgar was almost obsequious.

Howard was pretty happy with everything. He had vindicated his reputation, and the rights of all defense lawyers. Within a few short weeks, he had forgotten all about Rick.

A few days before Rick had reported to jail he went to Howard's office to settle up and say goodbye. He felt that there should have been more of a sense of nostalgia and a fond farewell coming from Howard and Viola after the shared time together over many weeks. After all, Rick was suffering and Howard was receiving money.

Hoping for some emotion before he left, Rick engaged Viola in conversation. To his surprise she was courteous almost to talkative and gave him a genuine smile as he walked out the door. Viola was sincerely happy, for she thought, *Adios thief. I shop at the Lucky Seven and I am tired of paying for people like you. You are just one less crook that I have to double-bolt my front door against. A wimp like you should be popular in jail.* She even gave him a big wave goodbye from behind the Plexiglas.

COLLECTIONS

Adelaide Schmidt was an artist. From grade school forward she excelled at drawing. She had been a precocious student and did well in most subjects, but sketching was her driving passion throughout childhood. During her junior year in high school, she spent a week learning sculpture in a studio downtown and was immediately hooked. She loved working with her hands and finding the forms inside the clay. Within a couple years her room was filled with sculptures that even to the untrained eye were wonderful expressions of form and movement. She took a fourth place ribbon in a competition where she was by far the youngest entrant.

It should have been no surprise that Adelaide got a college scholarship and announced to her mother, Betty, that she would major in Fine Arts. Betty was not pleased.

Betty was a single mother and Adelaide was an only child. A drunk driver had killed Betty's husband and childhood sweetheart when Adelaide was 3. Mercifully, Betty had a bachelor's degree in education and a good job at the local public grade school. Betty worked hard and made a good life for her and Adelaide but she was deeply aware of how much of a struggle such a life could be. Life was hard enough for a woman, and to get such an impractical degree was bound to end badly.

It was not as simple as all that either. Betty had grown up in a different time as well. When she went to college the standard roles of teacher or nurse were still dominant. But as the years went by she saw higher education opening up for women. They were becoming lawyers or doctors or real estate brokers or going into business. She had seen ambitious young women all around her and lamented staying in teaching. She had long wanted a graduate degree that might provide a real income, but between her job and her daughter, there was nothing to be done but work hard and save.

Adelaide could have a different life though. She was sitting on a scholarship in a world that was open to anything. By studying art, she might as well throw all of that away. It was hard enough to survive as a teacher, but as an artist? Adelaide's chances of making good money, especially during the early years, as a sculptor were extremely remote. Worse, Betty did not really want to be a permanent mother, and would have liked to see her daughter get a life of her own. As much as Betty loved Adelaide she did not want her daughter moving in with her for financial reasons.

She tried to lean on Adelaide. *Why don't you get a degree you can use?*

But I can use my degree. Adelaide protested.

I just think you should at least be able to get a job when you graduate. Can't you just minor in art and get a major in something practical, like business?

But mom, Adelaide said, *That is just not who I am.*

Betty smoldered. *Who you are is someone who is going to struggle her entire life without even the benefits that I had as a teacher.*

Somehow or other, Betty's little family unit was going backwards instead of progressing with the new generation. Adelaide would only be able to raise a family if she married rich and she had said repeatedly that, *Money is not the important thing.* Betty never swore out loud, just occasionally in her mind. This was one of those times. *Then what the fuck is the important thing? You will not know until it is too late.*

Adelaide went off to college. During her first two years, she majored in fine arts and got good grades. Otherwise she focused her studies around French, English literature, and science. She would come home every few months and rave about how great college was, and it took Betty every shred of emotional restraint that she had not to say, *Really? Shit. That is just great! What are you going to do with this in two years?* Maybe she could go to law school. Plenty of arts majors called that a fall back, right?

When Adelaide came home following her sophomore year, Betty could take no more. She was within a few years of retiring and understood that with Social Security and her retirement she could be comfortable. But she wanted so much more for Adelaide than to be comfortable. She certainly did not want Adelaide to have to marry for financial security or constantly be coming to Betty for handouts.

One beautiful summer afternoon, Betty exploded.

I cannot keep paying just to see you throw your life away! I'm sorry, but if you want me to continue to support you, then you need to change your major.

It was not necessary to say what the change should be. Both understood.

Adelaide took a deep breath and simply said, *Yes.*

She, of course, expected this and was almost relieved. As Adelaide approached her junior year, she began to understand that she would starve in the arts for a long time. She did not want to be a teacher, and the only other avenues were less appealing, and few of those would have required a four-year degree. She almost pitied her art teachers. Mostly they were unsuccessful artists who came back to teach and help others. They were just creative, talented people with spouses and children who found a financial life raft as a college instructor. The real world was much harsher than her raw talent and idealism could account for, and her mom just made the decision for her.

Adelaide got her BSBA and landed a job in the art museum. It was probably the combination of business and art that got her in, but at least it felt like a good compromise.

After a few years, Adelaide's old passions still had not died. She yearned to be creating art, not stuck in the administrative offices of the art museum. One day over lunch, it hit her: she could open an art gallery! With her savings and a small bank loan collateralized by a CD in Betty's name, Adelaide signed a three-year lease in the city's artistic district and opened Adelaide's Fine Arts. With her connections in the art world from her work at the museum, she was able to attract the artists she wanted, and had a good deal of control over what she could acquire. It felt like the beginning of the dream.

They say that experience is a dear teacher. Adelaide's experience was that her degree and time at the museum helped a lot, but they were not enough for her to make the business a success in the short term. She had set enough money aside to go six months without taking a full salary. She realized quickly that she should have planned more for eighteen months. She was able to pay her important debts like the bank loan and the lease, although she was frequently late, but credit cards, and some hospital and doctor bills, as well as a new transmission for her Subaru were piling up.

One such bill was to her doctor at Western Family Healthcare for $850.00. It had been an outstanding issue for some time, and eventually the accounts receivable department started threatening to send her to collections. Their voice message added that if Adelaide needed medical care in the future she should contact her county health department or go to a hospital emergency room. Despite these obvious Dickensian implications, Adelaide simply could not do anything about it. The money was not there. Adelaide felt a little ding to her self-worth. It was almost imperceptible, almost entirely subconscious, but yet there. For the first time in her life she experienced a situation that she would not be proud to tell her mother. It was not that Mom would say, *I told you so.* It was just so damn difficult to incrementally live a dying dream.

The collections agency called. Adelaide had never received a collections agency call in her entire twenty-seven years of life and was truly an innocent in the conversation. When she hung up about three minutes later the conversation had become a blur, but she realized that somehow, the stern-sounding lady on the other end had extracted a promise that Western Family's bill would be paid by the first of the month, or in about two weeks. Adelaide had not really meant to make a promise like that, but it seemed like the only way to end the call. Fielding calls from collections agencies was embarrassing and upsetting. Two weeks was a world away. A miracle or at least just a bit of good fortune could happen. She could sell something and get the commission. Her financial situation was so unpredictable; she might be awash in cash by then.

They did not call again for a while, though Adelaide did get a letter from Pacific Financial Resolutions, the collections company. The letter advised her of the debt and her right to dispute it. The back of the letter held a slab of legalese describing her rights in various states but it seemed to be no help. She did not, in fact, dispute the debt, so there was no point in saying she did. She noticed that the letter said that Pacific was a debt collector (surprise, surprise) and that anything Adelaide said would be used to collect her debt. It was kind of like the Miranda warning of the money police.

By the third week, she had managed to put most of this out of her mind. She had done enough business to pay both the lease and Betty's loan and was feeling pretty good. When her cell phone rang, she brightly answered, *Adelaide's Fine Arts, this is Adelaide.* More good news perhaps?

Her heart sank when she heard a woman with an antiseptic tone say, *Is this Adelaide Schmidt?*

She immediately had an almost overwhelming urge to say, *No,* but that was not who she was. On an intuitive level, Adelaide understood that this was not someone inquiring about artwork. This was the beginning of another conversation that she never wanted to have again. Another ding.

Miss Schmidt, this is Stephanie with Pacific Financial Resolutions, for security may I have the last four digits of your social security number?

Adelaide went silent trying to decide whether to comply and thought, *Hell, Stephanie knows she has the 'right person,' she called me I did not call her.* But she could not think of a really good reason to not comply and she knew that at the end she would comply and would have further prolonged the agony of the call. Adelaide complied. Another ding.

We did not receive your payment of $850.00 by the first of the month. Did you send it?

Adelaide thought, *You know damn well I did not send it. Had I sent it we would not be talking.* She even momentarily thought of saying, *Yes,* along with a little righteous indignation but realized it was just that fourth grade inclination to lie whenever caught guilty and that lying would probably make things worse.

She also knew that such a lie on top of the undone promise to pay would at best only keep the wolves away a few more days and in the follow-up call would actually give Stephanie the right to righteous indignation. Worse, it would eat at her. Adelaide always thought of herself as honest. In fact, she was trying to establish a reputation in the art world built on a small gallery of high integrity.

So instead, she just whispered, *No.*

My screen shows that you promised to pay by the first of the month, why didn't you send the money?

Even in this moment of crisis, Adelaide thought, *Your screen?* That sounds weirdly scripted. How does a person respond to that? Adelaide's screen only showed local artists.

I did not have it.

Why not?

I am self-employed and the money did not come in.

What do you do for a living?

I own an art gallery

Silence. Adelaide felt judged by that painful silence.

When will you have the money?

I do not know. Adelaide was being really honest with both Stephanie (and maybe for the first time since starting her business) with herself.

Do you intend to not pay your debt to Western Family Healthcare?

No, I intend to pay.

When?

She did not think that *I do not know* would go over too well, so

Adelaide said, *As soon as possible.*

When is that?

I can pay by the 20th" Adelaide would say anything to end this conversation. She actually had no idea when or how she would pay, but this conversation felt like it had gone on forever. Actually it had been a little less than ninety seconds.

Are you sure?

Yes.

How will you pay?

By check.

You can give me check information right now and we will hold it until the twentieth.

Oh shit no, Adelaide thought. Just what I need is a bad check to these people and the sheriff showing up at my door. *No thank you.* Stephanie gave up on that one pretty easy. Adelaide felt that Stephanie had decided it was time to move on to another call.

Allow enough time for mailing. I have marked your file that we will receive $850.00 by the 20th. I have placed a hold on reporting this debt to the credit service bureaus. If we do not receive payment in full by the 20th we will report you.

Understood. Good bye.

Adelaide, one more thing. I see we have your home and cell phone number. May I have your business number and address?

Adelaide remembered that when she first went to see Western Family about 5 years ago, she did not own the gallery. She complied and gave the information to Stephanie. Again, anything for this conversation to end.

Is there any more contact information for you?

No.

After hanging up on what was only a conversation of a couple minutes, Adelaide felt drained and humiliated. The last time that she could remember feeling like this had been in high school the one and only time she cheated on a test. Because she was an otherwise exemplary student and cried for half an hour straight in the principal's office, her punishment had been light. The worst thing about the experience though, was when they called her mother. That was the most important thing here: that bank loan had to be serviced. Adelaide's mother must never know about any of this. The loan guaranteed by Betty would always be paid on time and the bank would never be given a reason to contact her.

On the 20th of the month Adelaide sent a check to Pacific Resolutions for $425.00 and prayed that might placate them until she could send another. She had started screening her calls, and answering gingerly, hoping that she could avoid making contact. This worked well enough on her cell, but the business number did not have caller ID, so when it rang on the 25th, she just answered. *Adelaide's Fine Arts, this is Adelaide.* It is funny in life that as long as Adelaide was on her mental guard, she never got the Pacific call, but as soon as she let down . . .

Miss Schmidt, this is Edwina from Pacific Financial Resolutions. We have tried to call you many times but you have never gotten back to us. Adelaide knew that "many times" actually meant "twice". She marveled at how Pacific's reps could turn a business transaction into a social affront with a collections agency playing the role, of all things, the victim.

Why haven't you called?

Momentarily, Adelaide had the courage and frustration to offer a confrontational response, she replied, *I did not want to talk to you.*

Why not?

At that moment, for some unknown reason, Adelaide

remembered the Pacific letter. *You sent me a letter telling me not to talk to you or you would use it against me. So I am taking your advice.* Adelaide knew in her heart of hearts that this was a momentary victory, but it was still a victory and she basked in Edwina's silence on the line.

Edwina was momentarily thrown off her game. She heard the same lame dodges, excuses, cowardice, lies and profanity a hundred times a day. She had a response for every single one. She had never heard this one before, and she understood it was true. Pacific's letter basically did say that the conversation was meant to benefit Pacific and not Adelaide. There is a reason Pacific does the calling. They want to talk. They need to talk. Adelaide does not. Edwina fell back on her standard comeback when the conversation was headed in the wrong direction.

Don't you want to discuss your debt?

Discuss? What did that mean? Adelaide always thought of herself as someone willing to "discuss" anything that needed to be discussed. Of course Betty had raised the kind of reasonable person who would have a reasonable discussion upon a reasonable subject. Adelaide noticed that Betty's presence seemed to always lurk on the fringe of her thinking during these painful interludes.

But this discussion's request and demand were scary. Adelaide did not know what would happen if Edwina got mad. Could Adelaide be sued? Adelaide immediately regretted being flippant and terse. She resigned herself to the "discussion."

Okay, she said.

Miss Schmidt, twice you promised to pay your bill in full to Western Family and twice your broke your promise. You need to pay this bill now. Edwina was indignant and maybe a little wounded by Adelaide's two lies. She was also a little pissed at being caught off guard by an obvious novice debtor. Edwina sounded as though this was her money and as though Adelaide was a recalcitrant child who had hidden it somewhere.

I can't.

Why not?

I do not have the money right now.

Throughout these talks Adelaide half way thought that she would give an answer that would cause Edwina to end the conversation like, *I don't have the money.* Adelaide was wrong. Edwina did not get paid to retreat.

When will you have it?

I do not know, probably by the end of the month.

I can't accept that. You need to pay this debt now. Your doctor did his part and now you need to pay your debt. You have twice promised that you would pay in full and you did not. Do you have a credit card that you can put this on?

No.

You do not have a credit card?

I do, but it is maxed out. Then she thought to herself, *God, please let this end!*

How are you going to pay? I need to know now. Do I need to get my supervisor on the line?

This was a new threat and completely out of left field. It took Adelaide entirely by surprise. The thought of starting all over with someone else at Pacific, someone who probably made Edwina look like a cherub, was more than Adelaide could take.

No please do not do that. I will borrow the money and send it in a week.

You will send all $440.00?

Well, at least they acknowledge my payment. $440.00? Oh, interest, thought Adelaide. *Yes,* she said.

How?

By check.

Will you use the same account as your $425.00 payment?

Yes.

OK, that is not acceptable. I want you to send in the $440.00 check today and post-date it for one week. Can you do that?

Yes.

OK, it needs to go out today. If I have it in two days I will not report you to the credit service bureaus.

OK, thank you. Then she thought to herself, *Did I really just say thank you?*

Adelaide almost took the phone from her ear when she heard Edwina say, *I want to update our records. Do you have any new contact information?*

No, she said, while really thinking, *I've learned my lesson on that one at least.*

Is Adelaide's Fine Art your only employer?

Yes.

How much do you make?

I do not want to discuss that. Adelaide got a spark of new-found courage. It was mostly that the humiliation had to stop.

Okay, just be sure the check goes in the mail today.

Okay.

Of course, Edwina was the supervisor. Her job was to follow up with any client that had already been contacted twice but still had not paid. And in fact, Pacific Financial Resolutions had long since reported Adelaide to the credit reporting agencies. They did this with anyone who had not paid within thirty days, but it took a while to appear. Using such a statement as a threat was a good way of driving less cooperative subjects into compliance.

Once they figured out that the report had actually been made, most of them forgot it. It was not worth complaining about. They really did owe the debt so on some level, Edwina's lie told the truth.

Over lunch Edwina regaled the junior reps with Adelaide's story. It was an object lesson in manipulating payment out of a debtor. But the best part of the story was when Adelaide had said "Thank you."

Yeah, Edwina laughed over her salad and Diet Coke until she snorted, *She thanked me for giving her ten minutes of shit. Really. And, get this, she owns an art gallery. What a loser, but thank goodness for people like her. They make this job fun and eventually they do pay.*

Edwina was a single mother of two who had a full time job and worked part time at Pacific. She had been raised in difficult times and had no problem with putting on an angry aggressive persona. It was how she had gotten through her childhood. She was really not a bad person, but she was a survivor and had no sympathy for a lying "good girl" like Adelaide.

Adelaide never did send the post-dated check. She simply did not have the time to deal with it, and figured she could overnight it or something later in the week.

Two days later, Adelaide got a call from her mom. After a brief back and forth, Betty asked, *Who is Pacific Finance Resolutions?*

Adelaide was stunned and speechless. Immediately she felt like a seven year old again. After a brief silence, she said, *It's a collections agency, why?*

Well some girl with a guy's name, I think it was Edwin, called. I did not recognize the number. It was an 800 number anyway so I assumed it was a solicitor. Anyhow, I listened to the message and Edwin said that I had a bill due to a place called Western Family Health and that she wanted to talk to me about payment. I've never been there, so I would have called her back and told her so, but I thought I heard her mention 'Adelaide,' so I called you first.

Adelaide's mind was on overload while trying to simultaneously process how Pacific even knew about her mother, and secondly and more importantly, how to answer her without crying. Adelaide decided to forget about the former question (it was too late to worry about that now), and focus on the latter. Adelaide just told the truth. Contrary to Edwina, Betty had raised a fine person.

Betty was amazingly kind and non-judgmental. She offered to lend Adelaide the money for the doctor's bill but said that a condition was that Adelaide needed to talk to someone, maybe a bankruptcy lawyer or a business lawyer, who could discuss the gallery and help determine if it had a realistic future. Adelaide said that she did not know anyone. She had done all the legal set-up of the gallery on her own. With her education and experience, she never imagined that she would need a business lawyer.

Fortunately her mom knew a guy named David. He had helped her with some estate planning, but he also did business law. Maybe he could help.

After they hung up, Adelaide felt more relieved than she had in years, but was still bothered by the question of how Pacific even knew Betty existed, much less how to get ahold of her. Then, a day or two later at 4:00 a.m., it hit her: when Adelaide first went to Western Family Healthcare, she had been twenty years old. The intake form required every patient under the age of twenty-one to give detailed contact information about the person "responsible for your bill." Adelaide had put down her mother's name and Western Family had dumped all of her data onto Pacific including the private contact information for her family. Adelaide thought, *What kind of a fucked-up family is Western?*

David was a good guy. Not only was he a fine business lawyer, but he also was a fine human being. On top of that he had survived his own financial difficulties and had dealt with collections agencies personally. He not only spoke as an attorney but also as one who could genuinely empathize with Adelaide's situation.

Adelaide made an appointment with David. They started with small talk about Betty and then went into Adelaide's general history. She explained how the gallery was profitable, but not enough to support her and pay her business and home bills. With her credit cards she could still make the minimum payments, but with the doctor's bill they had wanted everything now. She outlined her interactions with Pacific.

So, if you've paid them already, what do you need from me?

The income from Adelaide's Fine Arts is not going to magically double tomorrow, Adelaide said. *I now understand it will probably take one or two more years of work to make it reasonably profitable. I know I need to cut back on store hours and get a part time job, maybe with the museum, so that the entire burden of supporting me does not rest on my business. But I am not ready to abandon my dream. Hopefully I can make some changes that will keep me from having to deal with collections agencies in the future, but my fear remains, what if there is another Western Family experience? I cannot do that again, or at least if it does happen again, I want to know what to do about it. Can you talk to me about that? Can you help alleviate my fears if I ever go down this road again? I never want another experience like I had with Pacific.*

Of course. David leaned back in his chair, stared up and to the left, grabbed ahold of each related thought and prioritized them. *For a variety of reasons, not all of which are within your control, you might have to deal with a collections agency in the future. Let's talk about how to deal with that experience courageously and while preserving your dignity. The first thing that you need to understand is that the collections agency cares nothing for your dignity or anything about you as a person, they only want you to give up money as quickly and meekly as possible so they can move on to the next debtor. It is harsh and not something we want to admit even to ourselves, but all business is based upon two, and only two emotions, fear and greed.*

I don't know. I really don't think Adelaide's Fine Arts is only based on fear and greed. I think that I am using art to elevate my small part of the world.

Of course you are, but your business is not based upon 'elevation.' It is based upon sales. Have you ever awakened in the middle of the night worried about your business?

Only every other night.

Did any of your nocturnal concerns ever center on not loving your customers enough, not elevating their art experience enough, not making your artwork available enough by, say, lowering the price?

No, it centered on sales, bills, rent, Western Family and my mother's opinions and judgments about everything I have done once I decided not to go into teaching.

Of all those concerns, which was the deepest and strongest?

My mother.

Thank you for your candor. I did not mention that between fear and greed, fear is the stronger, as with you.

Now let's go over your interactions in detail from the beginning. To start with, how did Pacific know to call Betty? David could guess the answer but he wanted to hear it anyhow and he wanted Adelaide to hear her say it out loud.

Adelaide explained that she had listed Betty as the responsible party on her Western Family intake form some years before.

Doctor's offices make much of their 'privacy policies' and how they protect their patients. You might be tempted to think that this is because of their commitment to a higher ethical standard. It is not. Health organizations only have privacy policies because the federal government mandated it. Once you become sixty days past due, or whatever the doctor's accounts receivable standard is, they will automatically turn you over to their collections agency. And I promise you every doctor uses a collections agency. Do not think you are going to find a group of doctors that doesn't. Once they 'turn you over,' privacy goes out the window. They do not typically turn over treatment-specific records, but they will data dump whatever else they have got to, in your case, Pacific. In other words, they will give up all personal information about you. Remember when you filled out the intake form and it asked for all that contact and business information, and a copy of your driver's license? One reason they want all that information is to ensure that after they set the collectors on you, Pacific and the rest know exactly how to get ahold of you everywhere. When you owe a doctor money, all values related to the nobility of the profession go out the window.

Adelaide thought David sounded a little harsh about doctors in general. After all, she had been taught to respect them as the highest and most self-sacrificing profession, the best combination of compassion and wisdom, the best of altruism and skill. But another side of her was glad to finally hear someone confirm her sense that something was amiss in the ethical universe. David was putting words to that sinking feeling that came from the end of dream. She said, *Yes, I just felt throughout that Pacific was not the standard I thought a professional, like a doctor, would use. I understand that I needed to pay but I guess I expected better from my doctor.*

Adelaide, the days of 'your doctor' are pretty much dead. The doctor you are talking about was Betty's or maybe even her mother's doctor. But they are all gone. That kind of care and empathy is a thing of the past. Yes, doctors today are professionals and they help and save bodies and we need them, but the elevated standard to which you cling went out as the giant healthcare conglomerates along with insurance companies took control of the market. Now it is just another business, and doctors are businesspeople or more accurately the employees of businesspeople. On some level, it is not their fault. To operate a successful medical group practice, nice offices in the right part of town, the latest equipment, a large staff with at least one person solely dedicated to dealing with insurance and of course, the doctor's child support, all bear on the paramount nature of cash flow. But I hear you. We all miss the family physician in the Norman Rockwell paintings.

What did you mean by 'save bodies?' Doctors save lives, right? Adelaide was almost regretting she ever came to see David. He was starting to depress her and raise issues she did not come here to discuss. She wished he would just stick to playing the role of lawyer, and yet a part of her was fascinated by his clarity.

Doctors and hospitals and pharmaceutical companies talk about saving lives, but all they do is save bodies. The Christ, the Buddha, Isaiah, whatever your beliefs, they saved lives. The most a doctor can save is a body.

But why didn't I get more communication from Western Family before they turned me over to Pacific? I would have been happy to begin a payment schedule and maybe keep them as my medical provider. Why couldn't I just talk to a human being at Western who acted like a human being? Isn't that exactly the image doctors present? Adelaide was not quite ready to abandon the dream.

I am sure there is an internal financial protocol for deciding when to turn an account over, but as much as anything it comes down to the level of pressure on you and the decision to sue you. The doctor's office does not want to be seen as using the coercive, high-pressure techniques that a collections agency will use. Doctors want to keep their hands clean. Your doctors do not want you to be able to say that Western Family Healthcare was verbally abusive or high pressure or even simply less than honest. That opens the door for you to report them to the medical board or Channel 9 News. So they get a collections agency to be their shadow side. Pacific, on the other hand, wants to be known as tough, humorless and without pity when collecting. The shadow side of a medical clinic is the glory of a collections agency. Finally, when they sue you in court to collect and I assure you they would have sued you for the debt and their attorney fees as well (you signed a contract), it is Pacific that is now in charge of your debt. Pacific would have sued you rather than Western Family Healthcare. In the past, medical professionals had to sue in their own name, what is called the 'real party in interest.' But professional and business representatives lobbied the legislature so that the collections agency could handle the entire process and the doctor's name would not appear anywhere. Avoiding the bad press that comes from financially attacking someone whose body you just fixed, well that alone is worth the percentage that the collections agency takes for its work. The last thing Western Family wants is to have the average person walk into county court on his case and see a docket list on the wall of ten cases, each of which features Western Family Healthcare as the plaintiff. That would send the wrong message to the other 60 people on that same morning's docket about the meaning of 'family.' But a court docket of Pacific Financial Resolutions as plaintiff reveals nothing about the underlying creditor.

And it works well for them in other ways, too. Had you been married, they would have sued your husband, even though he was never involved with Western Family and never agreed to pay your bill, even if the two of you were separated. Again, someone lobbied the legislature for the right to sue spouses for medical bills. He would be part of the family. So Western Family can hide behind Pacific both in name and tactics. The medical profession is still invested in your belief that you are, in fact, dealing with your mother's doctor even though you are, as is now painfully obvious, not doing so.

A part of Adelaide continued to see David as a little too enthused about coming down hard on the medical profession (David might have conceded this - he had not been able to get into medical school and law was his second choice). She had really like her doctor at Western Family and was going to miss her. After a while, they were on a first name basis. She had even thought of suggesting that they get together socially. She had been going there for seven years after all. Adelaide wondered if her doctor would even notice after a while that Adelaide had stopped coming. Maybe she would wonder why, maybe even check on her. She wondered if her doctor understood what accounts receivable and Pacific Financial Resolutions was actually doing to patients. But as before it also did Adelaide good to hear someone else express some indignation at the way her situation had been handled. Adelaide knew she rightly owed the money, she just thought that she would have received something better (maybe the word is "honorable" or as David said, "noble") treatment at the hands of her doctor. As an honorable person herself, Adelaide understood that the doctor should have treated her with greater respect, not for her sake, but for the doctor's.

David then asked Adelaide to recount one of her conversations with Pacific so they could unpack it together, and as lawyers say, "get to clarity."

Adelaide's problems with Pacific had begun with her sense of safety. The idea that she said she never felt safe from their calls nagged at her. After all, Pacific had her home, cellphone, and business numbers. She was never safe from them. Anytime her cell or home popped up an 800 number or "unknown caller," Adelaide felt afraid of the caller. It was especially harrowing at work, where she did not have caller ID on the business landline. She could have gotten caller ID on that line, but it felt like cowardice and giving in to the collectors.

Well, that is easy enough to avoid in the future, said David. *Stop giving out your numbers so easily. In the future, when someone requests a contact number, use your business line.*

But the intake form requests each of home, business, and cell.

Write the same number down for all. Most of the time they will not even mention it. If someone does, just tell him or her that you use the same number for all three. I promise you that if you have health insurance they will take you on as a patient whatever numbers you write down. And, by the way, never put down anyone else's number. Do not list any other responsible parties. If they decide to put you into collections, you are just setting those people up for harassment.

But what about an emergency contact number?

What emergency occurs where the doctor needs to contact you? It is almost always the other way around. And in most of those cases, your general care provider will just tell you to go to the hospital emergency room. The only other time your doctor needs to contact you is with test results or appointment updates. That kind of thing occurs during office hours, so your business phone works just fine.

One more thing though, and I cannot emphasize this enough for your emotional wellbeing: be brave. Face down the dragon and answer their calls. You will notice that your days get better if you just deal with them. By law, they cannot contact you more than once a day, and while it seems like they want to keep you on the line forever, it will never be more than a few minutes. They have other fish to fry and do not really want to be on with you any longer than they have to. And, honestly, since you and I agree that you need to pay the bill anyway, dealing with them does do you a benefit. It keeps you moving towards a resolution. Ignoring the issue will not solve anything. I know it sounds crazy now, but you may reach the point where you do not mind talking to them.

At that point you will have slain the dragon.

Adelaide looked at him quizzically.

Adelaide, there is nothing a collections agency can really do to you and they know it. Eventually you will notice that you are breathing; you can still see and hear and talk; you can still eat what you like; you still sleep in the same bed; the birds still sing and your mother still loves you. When you open the door to your apartment it looks the same. And most important, your dog has not changed his opinion of you. There is nothing they can really do to you. They let you do the really dirty work of tearing yourself up over these things. They just start the process. Collections agencies know how to push your buttons and turn your own mind, your own fears, and your own insecurities against you. And don't forget, if they only have one number you do not need to worry every time your phone rings.

I know what you are thinking. You are thinking that you have already given out your home, cell, and business numbers many times. We can deal with that too. Get rid of your home phone, you do not need it. Then get a new cell number, tell the phone company you do not want your old calls forwarded and give the number out only to friends. Send a blast email to your family and friends telling them your new number. Done. David shrugged. *It is an easy way to put an end to these calls and control them in the future. Now let's talk about handling the calls.*

But David, it kind of scares me to just end the cell phone number I have had for ten years. I don't know why, it just does. I don't want to do it. All my friends know me by that number.

Good. That is a sign of courage when you do that thing that scares you because you know it will help you. When you first sat down you said you wanted to know how to deal with the Pacifics of world if the situation ever happens again. Courageous, albeit small, steps where you stand up for your own dignity even if your doctor won't, is one of those ways.

Now you notice I did not tell you to change your business phone. There is the obvious reason of course, but also it is OK to have one phone where 'the world, for better or worse' can reach you. Every bit as much as privatizing your personal cell number is courage, being open to the world under your business number is also courageous. The good news is that when you are done with work you are also done with the world to the extent that you choose. Also your business phone has the 'hold' button, right?

Right, so what?

Oh my dear Adelaide, the 'hold' button is for you what Pacific's ability to call you but show no calling number is for them. Occasionally, while you are speaking with a 'Pacific' tell them you need to look at something or get a drink of water or whatever and place the call on hold. Do you have music on hold?

The classical station.

Great. When you tell the collector you are going to put him or her on hold, do not wait for a comment, just do it. Hold does not need to be for long, maybe just for 15 seconds. They hate it but they cannot say you hung up on them. If you do that, they love to use it to show themselves as a victim the next time you speak. Instead, you just took a necessary pause, took a breather, gathered your thoughts, that is all.

But why would I do it. Why play that game?

You do it to show courage to them, and more importantly to your-self. You do it to take a level of control of the conversation from them and back to you. Notice that in all conversations with Pacific, as it will be with any future collectors, they control, they run the show, they drive the train. They decide when the conversation will begin, choosing the time and day to call, and then they direct the conversation to center to-tally on your commitment to pay and then, when they choose, they end the conversation. You always go along; you assume that if you cooperate and don't make waves, the conversation will end quicker.

Well won't it?

Yes, it probably will, but it also concludes with you feeling defeated, dejected, humiliated and already fearful of tomorrow or the next day when it might all play out the same all over again. That fear is one of their weapons. Why not let the conversation go 15 seconds longer and show them that you can put a break in it without being rude, any time you feel like it. You can break their rhythm and the choice is 100 percent yours. The game, as you say, is about giving you control and courage and imprinting upon your consciousness that you are already playing the game, their game: the game that in the course of your life they control you. Show them that you have control as well. Do it for you. I promise, you will hang up and smile. Now tell me about the first call.

Well, I do not really remember much about the first call at all, Adelaide began, *I kind of remember the second call. Stephanie from Pacific Financial Resolutions called and…*

Okay, let's stop right there for a moment. First, always remember that the first thing out of a collections caller's mouth is a lie.

What are you talking about?

I mean the lady's real name is not Stephanie. That is a lie. Of all the possible names the one name that is not her name is Stephanie. Now we know that they do that to protect themselves, just like using a P.O. box instead of a street address, but it can be helpful to understand that they always start with an easy lie. It is easy because they do it without thinking. In fact, you may have spoken to 'Stephanie' more than once, just under different names. I tell this to you for more than the obvious reason. They want you to believe that the situation, the transaction the two of you are engaged in, has a moral basis and you are the moral transgressor and they are on the moral high ground. Collections agencies would not recognize Virtue if they met her on the street. Their sole foundation is greed and fear, actually using fear to satisfy greed.

Yes you agreed to pay and yes Western Family upheld their end and yes you should pay them, but, as you say, you are happy to work out an arrangement to pay. Neither Western Family nor Pacific wants that. They want to use power to squeeze you.

Adelaide nodded.

David continued. *Now, the name Pacific Financial Resolutions sounds almost pleasant does it not? We all want a pleasant resolution of our financial problems, yes? If they called themselves the 'Fuck You, Give Us Your Money Company' you would immediately have your guard up, would you not? And more importantly, you would, almost intuitively, better understand how to deal with them. Pardon my language, but I am trying to make a point.*

I think you just did, but it is okay. I understand where you're going.

Good, said David. *Just do not forget if you ever deal with such a company again, FU is its real name. Whatever else they say, always keep that in mind. The friendly sounding name is meant to sell creditors on how easily they will be able to get money out of you. The easy financial resolution message is for Western Family, not you. But it also has the added benefit of not alarming you, the target. What happened next?*

Adelaide was starting to relax. The game was beginning to make sense, even if it was horrible. *Stephanie, well whoever, asked me if I had sent in the $850.00 and when I said no, she said her screen said that I had promised to send it and why had not I sent it?*

Let's break this down. First, Stephanie knew going in that you had not sent the payment. She wants to establish up front her moral domination and your moral inferiority in the discussion. The question was designed to put you immediately on the defensive. And this is a standard technique. You look at this call, as you do everything in your life, from a responsible perspective. Stephanie looks at the call as a way to manipulate you into payment. She is taking advantage of your common human decency to corner you in to confessing or lying out of desperation. Also, notice how she used the word 'promise.' They love to talk about promises because of the moral and social weight the concept carries. All that aside you did the right thing by immediately telling her the truth.

Why's that? Adelaide asked. *It sounds like they do not really care about that.*

I think it is better for you. On an integrity level, you want to be an honorable person and honorable people best express that standard when dealing with dishonorable people. On a practical level, lies compound one another, and you want to have the details straight in your head. That is easiest to do with the truth. Besides, Stephanie talked about her 'screen' next, meaning what was on the computer in front of her. They know full well what the status of payment is. But referring to the computer screen is a great technique on a number of levels. First, how do you argue with it? The information is right there in front of her. Once you agree to what the 'the screen' says, the balance of information is on her side. Worse, she has a record of previous conversations, and because they like to catch you at random and put you on the defensive, you probably did not think to write anything down. 'Stephanie' even gets to pretend to be the aggrieved party.

Adelaide cocked her head. *What do you mean?*

There is a reason you are never told you are speaking to the same person twice. They want the exchange to be personal only on your side, never theirs. Stephanie wants all the weight of the moral approbation of your failure to pay without being the human to whom you made the promise. If you were dealing with the first person in the second call, you might even be tempted to apologize for not sending the payment. Then your caller would be placed in an awkward position of having to deal with your apology as another human might. She might be inclined to forgive. But if you never talk to the same person twice, there is no one to receive your apology. It also helps keep the person on the other end of the phone from becoming personally involved with you. It helps their staff retain complete anonymity on a level of more than name and address - they can say anything and not be bound by a personal connection to you.

That is amazing. It actually did cross my mind to apologize, but it felt stupid to apologize to a computer screen, Adelaide said.

Exactly. Stephanie got the benefit of being the first caller with complete recall of that conversation without having the social weight of actually being that caller. You, on the other hand, would never even think of going to your computer and transcribing the call after you hung up, or even during the conversation, because you just wanted to get as far away from the event as possible. You do not want to dwell on it. But Pacific wants to record the bad moments in your life and use those to get you to pay.

Oh my gosh.

What next? Actually, let me guess: she asked you why you had not paid, as if that really mattered.

Yes.

'Why' is such an interesting word; especially if you are ashamed of the answer. Did you notice that you started feeling as though you were seven years old again and had been caught at something you should not have been doing?

Adelaide nodded and thought of her childhood. She had always tried to be well behaved.

Well, 'why' has the same effect when you are twenty-seven years old, too. It is an off-putting word. Even giving a truthful answer feels suspect and maybe not good enough. They want you to feel that even your honesty is not quite good enough. How did you respond?

I do not remember word for word, but I explained that I was self-employed and just did not have the money and would pay as soon as I could, but I did not know exactly when. I did not want to get caught making a promise that I might not be able to keep again. 'Why' makes you search for an answer you think will be acceptable to the questioner, not the honest one. My answer for the Pacific questioner was always that I would pay soon.

That was not nearly good enough, was it?

Adelaide nodded. *Right, she asked me, now that I think of it, in an almost wounded, surprised tone, if I intended to pay the debt. It felt like she wanted to determine if I was really of low character. That made me want to defend myself.*

Yes, her time is valuable and she had others to call, and you were getting off track, David said. *You were telling a very real, honest, human story. Stephanie had no time for that nonsense. She just needed to extract a commitment. You had let her know that you were not quite ready to commit to a payment on a certain date, so she did the next best thing: She got you to recommit to the debt. You said that you certainly intended to pay, right?*

Right again, and then I did go ahead and promise to pay by a certain date. Once I had, as you say, recommitted to the debt, there seemed to be nowhere else to go. I said that I would send them a check later that month.

Whoa. David help up a hand. *Did you send a check?*

Not for the entire amount, but yes. Adelaide felt a sinking sensation, another ding.

Never, ever, ever send a collections agency a check, not even a cashier's check unless it is the very final payment.

But I felt funny about giving them my credit card number, Adelaide protested, *I knew with a check I was at less risk. With a credit card I was afraid that they might take out more than the agreed amount or take money more than once without my consent. With a check I knew that all they got was what I sent. Plus I just did not trust whose hands my credit card number might fall into. As you say, collections agencies are not exactly known as virtuous.*

Nice turn of phrase, David thought. *You're catching on.* Then he said out loud, *Your reasoning was sound, but a check still has real problems, too. By giving them a check, you just handed 'the enemy' valuable information. You told Pacific where you bank and at least one of your account numbers. If they had sued you and gotten a judgment, which, no offense, they probably would have won if Betty had not paid it off, you made it easy for them to raid your accounts through garnishment. Even with a cashier's check or bank money order, they learn where you bank. But at least with those two you do not run the risk of bouncing a check on a bill collector.*

I assume they would redeposit?

No, David said with a slight smile. *They would not redeposit. Had you bounced a check on them, they would have had you not only as social reprobate, but with criminal implications as well. You can bet they would cheerily use that against you. A really vicious collections firm could use that single event to secure up to three times the amount of the debt in court. Usually they do not go that far, but what they could do is threaten you with serious action if you did not pay up within a day or two.*

Adelaide frowned. *Then how should I pay them?*

Money order, David said flatly. *Nothing ever except a money order. They will try to persuade you to use a credit card, but you should never do that. Use only a money order. Make a photocopy of it, and mail the money order at the post office. And be sure and pay the extra for proof of delivery.*

But I like the check because I get a picture of it when they deposit it. That is proof of payment, right?

True, but the photocopy of the money order along with your proof of delivery is pretty good proof too. After all, there is no benefit to you in buying a money order, filling in the name of Pacific and then not sending it. You are still out the money. David moved on. *Toward the end of the conversation, did Pacific ask you about other ways to get a hold of you?*

Why, yes! David was starting to sound like a mind reader to Adelaide.

Let me guess, the collector said, 'Are there other numbers you would like to give us to contact you?'

Yes again.

As though sensing her surprise, David said, *They all behave pretty much the same way. They know that you, unless you get belligerent or just hang up, will always behave in pretty much the same way. They never ask you for information at the beginning of the conversation because that is not the most important thing to them. What they really want is for you to pay now. Besides, in the beginning of the conversation, you might still retain some courage and self-worth. That makes it hard to extract extra information from you. By the end of the phone call, they have worn you down enough that you will comply with anything just to get off the phone. But remember you are complying with a request that essentially says, 'You need to give us additional avenues to harass you.' It is crazy, and they count on their ability to make you behave irrationally. Every single request is scripted and calculated to your disadvantage. When the collector turns from aggressive to more pleasant when she has what she wants do not be thankful. They are counting on that newfound relationship when they phrase the question of 'Would you like to give us more contact information?' You received a form letter from Pacific telling you that any information you gave them would be used against you, right?*

Right

Believe the letter. It is honest. The government made them write it. Of course, if things start getting to be too much, most people also do not realize that you can limit or terminate contact by sending a letter to them. Just mail or fax a letter saying which telephone numbers that they already have that you want them to stop using.

Does that actually work? asked Adelaide.

Most companies will comply, said David. *Only the worst will ignore your letter or say they never got it.*

Is there any recourse against those?

Not really, unfortunately. Technically you can lodge a complaint with the Secretary of State's office. The Secretary of State usually regulates bill collectors. But it will not do any good.

Why not?

Pacific would deny everything you say. And unless you state in your complaint that you do not owe the money, then you are just another deadbeat looking for a way out. This is nothing against the Secretary of State's office; as you can imagine, the part of their office that regulates bill collectors is going to be swamped with both real, legitimate complaints and by deadbeats looking for a way out. The department has to go through every one of those cases. To be frank, by the time they get around to you, you will probably have already paid the debt and not want to think about it anymore.

I can imagine that, yes, said Adelaide.

It all really boils down to three choices. You can pay the debt, file bankruptcy, or just ignore them until they sue or go away. If Betty had not paid, I would have advised you to go for a version of that last option. Obviously yours is not a bankruptcy case. I would have said to send Pacific a letter telling them to 'Cease All Contact' and verbally tell them the same the next time they call. Now to be clear, in the letter also tell them you will send them $150.00 a month on the eighth of the month or whatever and be really good about picking an amount you know you can pay and then sending it on time. That would have been my advice. It probably would have solved it. By the way, they never *really go away. The report on your credit for the unpaid debt to Western Family would have remained even if they stopped contacting you and did not sue. At some point when you went to buy a house or a car the lender would have forced you to pay Pacific before they lent you money.*

David paused, turning the situation over in his head for a moment. *This really brings us to what this is all about, not only on a legal level, but a human one as well. Did you notice that after each conversation you were still breathing?*

Adelaide shook her head. *You brought this up before. I heard you but I was not certain that I believed you.*

Adelaide, that was your own insecurity. I read it on your face and that is why I am bringing it up again. After each conversation you were still breathing, still standing, still had two hands, still could laugh at a joke, walk around, talk to customers, tell your Mother you love her, smile at your puppy. David smiled. *Did you notice that all the things that really count in your life did not change one bit as a result of the conversations with Pacific? Did you notice there was nothing Pacific could really do to you? They depend on what's in your head to get compliance. That is why they promise to hold off calling you like it is some sort of favor. As I said before, they know what scares you. They are like the dark force in the horror movie that knows what scares you. Once you bring yourself to a place where you no longer care if they call or not, then they have lost their authority. One more thing to remember, and it is a good perspective to bear in mind: these concerns are what my twenty-something daughter refers to as 'First World problems.' No disrespect to you, of course, but never forget that 90 percent of the world would give almost anything to be you, Pacific and all.*

I know.

Now, if you can, step back from the situation, the whole collections phone call process and look back. Notice that Pacific never really had anything to say.

What do you mean?

I mean that they have no power without responses from you. If you were to say to a Pacific representative that you would have been happy to listen to anything they had to say, but that you would not engage in question and answer (which would be a reasonable and polite position to take), the call would be over. They are nothing without their questions and your tacit agreement to answer. They exist in a complete vacuum. If you wish, stop engaging in the non-conversation. That would turn the bill collector into what it really is, an apparition who disappears when you allow yourself to ignore it. You can use this tool at any time in the conversation. Of course, if you are dealing with a bill you want to resolve, then tell them what they want to know. Just stop when you are ready, and politely end the conversation. Simply say that you are done answering questions, but you will be happy to listen to any statements they wish to make. They will, in short order, hang up on you. Just stick to your position. They'll keep asking questions until they realize you have nothing more to say. And then they will stop to move on to someone more compliant. Also, remember, that while they will sue, they much prefer to keep the payments in house.

Wow.

Is there anything else you would like to discuss? David asked. It felt like he had given all the advice he could.

Well, it is actually funny that you use that word, said Adelaide. *On at least two of the calls Pacific said that they called to 'discuss' my account. Yet it sure did not feel like a discussion.*

It felt like a question and answer session, or even interrogation didn't it? In fact, they would just keep asking the same questions and trying to find discrepancies in your answers. If you said you did not want to answer a question they would either ask 'why,' as we discussed, or they would wait a minute and come back and ask it again. They are just trying to wring guilty commitments out of you. In point of fact, you probably never 'discussed' anything did you?

No.

'Discuss' is a socially polite word. Any reasonable person is willing to 'discuss' something, even if it is unpleasant. You view yourself as a reasonable person and so you agreed to 'discuss.' Again, they are using the word to manipulate your basic decency. All they really have to use against you is you. They are not going to send someone to beat you up. There is no such thing as debtor's prison. Your life is not a Dickens novel. Their main weapon is you, yourself.

Adelaide sighed. *That seems a terrible way treat people.*

It probably is. Just remember what you are dealing with when collections agencies call. It is not fair to call them evil, but they are soulless. You are essentially talking to a rock that wants something from you. A rock cannot relate to your humanity and neither can a collections agency. You are, as the Bible says, 'casting your pearls before swine' when you count on your common humanity to help you through encounters with collections representatives. While they would like to make you feel morally inferior, in reality, as long as you do not get mad, do not get afraid, tell the truth, and act with courtesy and dignity, you are in the superior position. Once they have asked you the same question twice, tell them so. And tell them they already have the best answer. Do not let them manipulate you into making commitments that you are not certain you can fulfill. The Pacifics of the world will say anything they can get away with to get you to pay. Do not be like them. Do not just say anything to get them to go away. And remember that the truth is always your best friend. In the end, this debt, like any debt will be meaningless. But your conduct and your confidence in your own self-worth will be recorded in your understanding of who you are. Hold your head high. You are a fine human being, and nothing that a Pacific or any other bill collector can do will ever change that, unless you let them.

I guess when we remove the money, what really hurts is how my doctor of eight years could send me to such people. Maybe she did not really know what's going on with them?

Sorry, dear Adelaide. She knows, she knows.

HOW TO FIND, INTERVIEW, HIRE AND FIRE A LAWYER

FINDING

The traditional method of referral remains the best way to locate a lawyer. Find someone who describes his or her lawyer as "wonderful, great, etc." Even if that lawyer does not practice in the area in which you need help, you might call her anyway and see if she knows someone, or knows someone who knows someone. Competent, friendly compassionate lawyers attract similar lawyers as acquaintances.

If you cannot find someone by referral then try the Internet. If you do not have a solid referral, interview several lawyers and realize that you are likely to fall victim to the human tendency to hire the last one. There is a reason automobile dealers tell you to shop them last. Do not tell later lawyers what the earlier ones were going to charge you. The latter will just undercut the earlier to get your business and that is no criteria to hire someone. Potentially just the opposite is true.

If you get a professional referral from your CPA, financial planner, etc., get at least three referrals. The fact that your financial planner has a long-standing personal relationship with a lawyer, where each sends all his business to the other, is a terrible reason to hire a lawyer. Ideally still, find a friend with a recommendation. When you interview the lawyers referred from the CPA or planner do not be shy about asking the lawyer about his relationship with the CPA or planner.

You can go to the Supreme Court Attorney website and look at the disciplinary history of any lawyer you are considering. But do not let an incident necessarily put you off. There a many reasons that a lawyer might have disciplinary action taken that do not necessarily mean she is a poor choice.

Understand whether you will have a long-term relationship with the lawyer on not. The lawyer understands this very well. Business lawyers, estate planning lawyers, real estate lawyers are examples of lawyers that you may well work with again over the years. Bankruptcy, divorce and criminal are examples of lawyers that (I hope for your sake) you will only deal with once.

Understand that in those cases, particularly with bankruptcy and divorce, you are on an assembly line. That is no criticism of either side, just the truth. That truth is compounded by the fact that neither you nor your lawyer will ever want to see the other again once your business is over. You will not want to see your lawyer because she is a walking remembrance of a very difficult (if not the most difficult) time in your life. Your lawyer will not want to see you because she dealt with you at one of your lowest emotional points and that is her memory of you. Your lawyer understands this with crystal clarity. It is important that you do as well. So get on the assembly line and get it over with.

Most lawyers will offer a free consultation for each of you to judge the other. It is usually listed as half or an hour. If the conversation goes beyond an interview and turns into the lawyer actually giving legal advice you should expect to pay. But the lawyer should let you know when the charges begin with something like, *Can we go on the clock now?* Do not go see a lawyer just because she advertises a "free consultation." Virtually all lawyers do that. It's like when an automotive shop offers a "Free 12 Point Checkup." It is just intended to get you in the door.

There is an exception. Most divorce lawyers will want you to pay, usually one hour of their time, for an initial consultation. Their reasoning is that otherwise they could literally spend all of their time in free consultations. Additionally, a divorce consultation is unlike any other in its emotional intensity. The divorce lawyer (correctly so) believes that if she has to hear an hour about what a jerk your soon to be ex-husband is, then she should get paid. Even in a non-divorce situation, if the lawyer wants to be paid for the first hour that should not deter you from going.

You should be able to get in to see a lawyer for an interview within ten business days, usually sooner. If the time is longer than that (and she is not on her extended yearly vacation) then that lawyer is probably too busy for you and things will not be handled as expeditiously as you would like in the future. She is not going to change. The only other exception would be a litigation attorney who is in a two week to month long trial. Such trials are all consuming and the lawyer will drop everything to focus on that trial. On the other hand, if your litigation case is not of a magnitude that it merits the attention of the kind of attorneys who do month long trials, then you are talking to the wrong (spelled "too expensive") guy to begin with.

When you make your calls to schedule the initial consultation appointment have your antenna up from the start. Do you have to go through the general receptionist and the lawyer's secretary to talk to him? While not a criticism, understand that you will have to do so every time you call if you hire him. In many of the finest law firms, the lawyer will have a direct line number (which you will have) that she will answer herself if she is available. That is an excellent way to keep you happy and the lawyer responsible. You know that she is there for you when you need (of course at her hourly rate) and the lawyer must be attentive enough to your case that she is comfortable talking to you "cold" whenever you call.

Listen carefully to both spoken and unspoken communications from the staff. If the receptionist acts swamped (immediately puts you on hold for more than 30 seconds), if the lawyer's assistant's tone of voice or sighs or briskness indicate that she really does not want to be there, then YOU really do not want to be there either. Do not make the appointment. Get off the phone and cross that lawyer off your list. No one knows more about the mood and productivity of a law firm than staff.

THE INTERVIEW

With regard to the interview, have your antenna up and fully aware from the moment you pull in the parking lot. Speaking of which, be aware of little things. If you have to pay to park (though usually parking is comped), or if you have to pay to park and it's a hike to the office, you will do that every time you see your lawyer. In some cases you will only need to see your lawyer once or twice so it does not really matter. But if you will become best friends (well, best acquaintances) with your lawyer for a while (divorce, litigation, etc.) the park and hike can get old.

Observe the office waiting area with an understanding, but not judgmental eye. Keep in mind that both the lawyer and the staff understand that the waiting area is the critical first impression. If the area does not give a good first impression, then you know that, on some level, the lawyer and staff do not care about your first impression. This is not a good start. Many lawyer offices are beautiful but all of them need not be. They need to be clean (plants, if fake, dusted) and orderly. There should never be any indication of any client's work visible from the waiting area. A client's work should not be in the conference room (which you can probably see from the waiting room) unless there is a human being also in there working on it. A simple and clean, but not pretentious, waiting area can be the waiting area of a fine law firm. A disorganized, dusty waiting area with old furniture and pictures can be a sign of what's to come. The current day's newspaper in the waiting area is a good sign. If the area is full of awards and recognitions, that can be a warning sign. Similarly, if the lawyer is anxious for you to know that he was an Eagle Scout or is a Christian or if all of the family pictures on his desk face you and not him, consider why he is using what should be altruistic endeavors to promote himself. The lawyer's primary concern is supposed to be you, not self-admiration, or worse, using that as a marketing tool.

Is the receptionist engaged with what he is doing? If he is not, it can be the sign of several things. It can be a sign of marginal training - literally of just taking the applicant and showing him how to use the phone system one morning and throwing him behind the desk. That suggests a lack of care. It also can be a sign of a lack of cohesiveness (understanding of the common goal) among the staff, which also is a lack of care by the attorney. Every action, every call, every piece of paper, every word in a law office has one, and only one, primary goal: the best interest of the clients. If staff does not understand, that is the fault of the lawyer. Again, she does not care. Finally, an apparently unengaged receptionist can have all the training and care in the world, but if he is underpaid he will not perform. The client actively wants everyone who works at her lawyer's office to be well paid. I will say it again. You actively want the staff at your lawyer's office to be well paid. A lawyer can pick and choose the best people (both in personality and competency) if he is paying an above normal wage. If they are well paid, they value their jobs and thereby value the client. Underpaid staff will never care as much as they could. No amount of training will solve that. Underpayment also shows an elevated level of avarice in the lawyer, which will affect many of his relationships with his clients and create a high turnover in staff. That is clearly not to your advantage.

You should not wait any longer than 15 minutes to see the lawyer. If it is a long wait, he will always have an excuse about how busy he is. That is an insight for you in the first 30 seconds with him about his time management skills. Emergencies happen, but on a daily basis, one client's case should never, ever impact another client's case.

Note if he takes you to his office or to a conference room. There is nothing wrong with meeting in the conference room. Frequently it is the nicest large area in the suite. But it can also be that the lawyer does not want you to see his office because it is a pit.

If you meet in his office, take a moment and look around. You will learn volumes. Does it look like someone took care with decorating or is it haphazard? Ideally, somewhere in the office is a picture of his family. Take note if the direction of the picture is to remind him of what he values or it is primarily a silent marketing tool. Beware of the office that is self-aggrandizement overkill: diplomas, certificates, Eagle Scout awards, Rotary Awards, etc. There is nothing wrong with displaying honors but be intuitively aware that you may be really dealing with a 14 year old in a 40 year old body seeking the approval of the world.

There is another important visual in the office: files. Are files lying about? That alone is not necessarily bad, particularly with guys and gals who spend a lot of time in court. Their offices will frequently have large files. The real question is whether they are the small group of files the attorney is working on or whether his credenza, desk and floor have become the de facto resting place for his clients because he is too lazy, distracted, disorganized, compulsively controlling or overwhelmed either by his practice or his life outside the practice to put them away or have someone else do it. On some even deeper level, the disdain with which the lawyer treats a client's paperwork is telling about his feelings for the client.

Once seated it is the lawyer's obligation to lead the conversation. He should begin by telling you about himself. Personal details are good. Listen for crisis. Recently divorced? Other personal problems? You cannot really ask about them but most humans will talk. He should then move over into generally the kind of law he practices.

First let's begin with questions that are not worth asking. Examples are, "Where did you go to law school? What was your class rank? How many times did you take the bar?" I have known brilliant, successful lawyers who went to third tier law schools, did not rank well or win any awards and took the bar more than once. The guy or gal may simply have a rebellious personality and most of us understand that the standards of academia and the standards of life are often unrelated. Similarly, the lawyer who went to a great law school, had a high class rank and won awards may have had a father who could not say "I love you" and the 14 year old stuck in a forty year old lawyer's body is still trying to win his father's approval.

CLIENT QUESTIONS

1. **How long have you practiced law?** It's OK if the person has not practiced Law very long if a senior lawyer supervises her. Similarly a lawyer who has practiced for a long time might already be mentally retired with only his body showing up at work.

2. **What percentage of your currently active cases are cases like mine?** Less than fifty percent is OK, but your case should be in an area that the lawyer devotes at least twenty-five percent of her time. Throughout the questioning, always remember that body language and facial expression are as important as words.

3. **What is easy about my case?**

4. **What is difficult about my case?**

5. **Do you return all client communications (telephone calls, Emails, faxes) the same day?** Within twenty-four hours? Ever? Do you have a preference for communication? Many older lawyers, if you ask, will tell you that they are

not comfortable with electronic communications. On its face that is easily handled but it may also tell you something about the lawyer's stage in career that you may find unappealing.

6. **What do you expect the price range of my case to be?**

- The lawyer will have all kinds of conditions and not be able to "predict the future" in his answer, but he should be able to give a reasonable range. The answer should include everything: attorney fees, paralegal fees and costs. Do not ever expect that the ultimate price will ever be at the low end, but it should not surpass the high end without a really good reason that you learn about at the time of your interview. This range is by far the better key to cost rather than hourly.

- Many cases, such as estate planning, are handled on a flat fee basis. E.g. there is a set fee for a will or a trust. This is a good way to work, but never pay more than half up front as a retainer. A lawyer who needs to accomplish the work to get paid is incentivized. A lawyer who is already paid is not.

- Contingency fees are fees where the lawyer only gets paid if you do. Although you usually owe for costs, win or lose. They are fine for personal injury and collection of child support and other debts where the outcome is uncertain and the lawyer shares the risk. Contingency fees are an abomination in probate and cases where the outcome is not uncertain, in other words, where nothing is contingent. Run away from those lawyers.

7. **Firms will often have stepped hourly billing rates.** Senior
partner is $500.00 per hour, associate is $200.00 per hour,
and legal assistant (formerly paralegal) is $100.00 per hour.
At the interview with the senior partner, he will use as a
selling technique the fact that he will only be involved to
review and give advice on major decisions, and most of the
legal work will be done by the associate, and "paperwork"
by the legal assistant. Legal secretaries used to be part of
the lawyer's hourly billing but then lawyers learned that the
legal secretary could be elevated to "legal assistant" at a decent hourly rate while still paying her $25.00 an hour. But
here is where Question 6a is so important and what stepped
hourly firms sometimes do to increase billable hours. Every
time the two or three players at the firm talk to each other
about your case they combine their billing. If once a week
all three meet, you are paying an effective $900.00 an hour.

Understand that lawyers at medium to large firms are
under tremendous pressure to bill. Let's take a simple example. In Denver, a new graduate who did well in school
will expect to make $100,000.00 per year plus benefits. In
fairness, she may well have large student loans. She paid
$50,000.00 a year for three years to go to law school. A sal-
ary of $100,000.00 per year plus benefits and payroll taxes
is say, a $140,000.00 a year cost to the firm. That means
she must collect (not just bill) at least $280,000.00 a year
to be worth it. If she works fifty weeks a year, then she
must collect $5,600.00 a week. If she works five and a half
days a week that comes out almost exactly to $1,000.00
a day every day without fail. Miss a day and tomorrow is
$2,000.00. Take your child to her soccer game on Saturday

morning then you are down $600.00 if you don't work Saturday afternoon. That means she must bill and collect five hours a day. In working eight to ten hours a day, five billable/collectable hours is about right. These figures and these thoughts are never far from your lawyer's mind.

8. **Do you bill for essentially clerical matters?** For example, do you bill if I call to confirm a court time? Or to simply forward a letter from someone else? Or worse, for your own time spent reviewing billing?

9. **In what increments of time do you bill?** Five minutes? Ten minutes? Fifteen minutes? Does that mean a thirty-second conversation will be billed for ten minutes?

10. **Will I spend most of my time talking about my case with you?** Your junior associate? Your legal assistant? The temp receptionist?

11. **Now, you already know whether the lawyer has ever had a bar complaint because you went to the Supreme Court website and looked her up before the interview.** If there are one or two complaints (never, ever any more than two) it's OK, if you think you otherwise like her, to bring it up and ask what happened. The lawyer may be initially surprised but she should be willing to candidly discuss it. Most lawyers will have a reason why it is not their fault and that's OK if you believe them. If you do not believe her, then the interview is over. Trust your intuition. I say again, trust your intuition, it will not fail you. Assuming the infraction was not egregious, if the lawyer simply confesses that she made a mistake, this may be a fine human being you should consider hiring.

12. **Is there anything about my case, your practice or you personally that I have not asked about (or do not even know to ask about) that you ought to tell me?**

13. **Do you really love what you do?** (Reader, I assure you that he or she has never been asked this question before by a client, or probably anyone else, since those with a familial stake in the response do not necessarily want to know the answer. "I really want to open a flower shop" may well spell divorce.) Forget the verbal answer. The body language and facial expression will tell you all that you need to know (and I regret that I cannot be with you to see it).

There is no right or wrong answer. The questions are geared more to keep you from being surprised, set the ground rules, and help you find someone you like and are at least are in sync with. (But remember all of the answers when you are editing the lawyer's engagement letter). The famous trial attorney, Clarence Darrow, had a list of rules by which to know whether to exclude a potential juror. But he said that you could forget the rules if you could find someone who laughs. Similarly, the most important question and answer in the list are at number thirteen. She should be smiling and laughing when she answers.

The lawyer should not take calls during the interview unless he explained up front that there is one call he cannot miss (like from a judge). The lawyer should be entirely engaged with you during the interview. If he takes notes, so much the better.

Do you like her? Does she seem genuine? Has she given you clues, both spoken and unspoken, that are positive or negative? It is said that we hire ourselves. There is much truth to that statement.

Be aware of it and be aware that in your particular case, your own personality may not be the best to accomplish what you would like.

Finally, if you interview three lawyers (which you probably should) do not tell lawyers two and three anything about your earlier interviews or that they even occurred. You give the later lawyers an unfair advantage if they understand the terms of the earlier conversations. Let each one stand on his or her merits alone.

HIRING

Hiring is important. It is more than just selecting a lawyer. The lawyer is going to want a retainer. A normal retainer will be in the $2,500.00 to $5,000.00 range. A retainer is a sum of money that the lawyer will keep and bill against.

There are two types of retainers. With the first, after the law firm has spent the initial $2,500.00, it will begin to bill you monthly for the amount owed for the previous month. Actually, the firm will bill you monthly from the start, but each bill will reflect the reduction in your retainer for the amount used for legal services that month. With the second, each time the retainer is gone, or almost gone, the firm will ask you to "replenish" it and give them another $2,500.00. This is a way for the law firm to make sure that it never gets two or three months behind in your payments, and worse, after those three months you leave and do not pay.

In addition to payment, retainers serve another very important function to the law firm and indirectly to the client. Retainers are gauges of sincerity and commitment. Clients frequently express righteous indignation at the soundness of their cause or their desire to accomplish some end but writing a five figure check is an easy, simple test to determine how truly indignant or desirous they are.

With the possible exception of estate planning, very little in the legal field moves forward without an expectation of personal gain regardless of the moral issue. Even the people who sue large companies to set an example or see to it "that this never happens again or never happens to anyone else" usually keep the money rather than use it to set up a mechanism to see to it that this never happens again. Even estate planning is not altruistic. It buys peace of mind for the planner.

Once the two of you have agreed on a retainer (which means you have agreed to pay your lawyer's requested retainer), the firm will send you an "engagement letter." Not nearly as pleasant as a real "engagement," this letter outlines the rules of your relationship. It initially gives the impression that it is written to balance the interests of both sides. It is actually written to protect the interests of the law firm while giving you the rights that the state Supreme Court says you, as client, were entitled to even without the letter.

The engagement letter is a pre-existing form in which the lawyer's assistant has filled in your name, an outline of your project, and the hourly rates being charged. It also states that either of you can quit, but you still have to pay the remainder of your bill in the case of the first style retainer. In the case of the second (or in the case of the first if you quit early on), if you decide to quit, the firm is required to refund the balance of your retainer. Having said that, you may note in real life that a law firm has an almost religious reluctance to see money flow the "wrong way" and its final bill will reflect an attempt to legitimately keep as much of the retainer as possible.

Keep in mind that in the vast majority of cases you have many choices as to who will be your lawyer and so that means that the engagement letter is negotiable within certain limits. Most attorneys will not negotiate their fees, although it never hurts to try and you might be surprised at the outcome. One example of what you can negotiate is copying your file for the use of your next lawyer, or yourself. Old firms will want to charge for that. You might want to put in the engagement letter that such final copying is free. In a backwards way, technically the law firm's file is already yours, but copies are not. When quitting, always ask for your file, not a copy of your file. If the firm wants to copy the file for its records, then it is responsible for the cost.

This brings up another important point. In law it's really good to understand which agreements are negotiable and which are not. There remains from the 1800s a nostalgic remembrance of the agreement negotiated at arm's length by two equal parties who come to a balanced contract and move forward with it. That is a dream of a time long gone that has nothing to do with the contracts signed by the average person today. Agreements for insurance, cell equipment and service, purchasing a car (except for the price), cable TV, obtaining a credit card, etc., are never negotiated. You may take them or leave them. Going to another credit card company or insurance company is no help. The underlying agreement is always the same. Even if you get a "deal," it is always offered by the company and not as a result of your request. It has gotten to the point where no one even reads those agreements because reading and understanding them changes nothing, and just depresses and confuses you.

You will note in the agreement that there is an arbitration clause. Like engagement letter, arbitration has a much more cooperative ring to it than its reality proves. The aura of arbitration, when it first appeared strongly on the legal scene in the 1980s, was that it was a faster, cheaper, easier, friendlier way for citizens to resolve issues than the backlogged, pompous system of courts. But as time went on, large companies, or the side in the position of power in the agreement, learned that arbitration is exactly what was needed to keep the other side (usually the average person) at a disadvantage should a complaint arise. There is a reason why insurance contracts have an arbitration clause. It is not so that it will be faster, cheaper, easier, and friendlier for you to make a complaint against the insurance company. There is a reason why your landlord has an arbitration clause in your lease. It is not so that it will be faster, cheaper, easier and friendlier for you to make a complaint against him regarding your apartment or his failure to perform. The lawyers who wrote the lease form that the landlord is using did so to set up a barrier to protect him from you.

Here is what the side in power learned about arbitration clauses. By the way, the strength of the side in power can be as simple as the fact that you have nowhere else to go where there will not be an arbitration clause. If all engagement letters have them, then the law firm, regardless how small, is the side in power. Firms learned that initially (which is where the complaint deterrent is most effective), arbitration is much more expensive than filing a lawsuit. While a jury trial might be two or three times as expensive as arbitration, the price of admission to get into arbitration is much more expensive than a court filing. In Colorado, the fee to file a district court case without a jury is around $200.00 and with a jury is around $400.00. The minimum fee to file an arbitration case with the American Arbitration Association is $1,000.00 and the fee is based on a sliding scale. The more money you want as a result of your injury (you greedy little complainer you) the higher the price of admission, and it can go really high. This fee will prove to be a major deterrent to making a legal complaint unless the law firm's conduct was truly egregious.

I n arbitration there is no trial by jury, limited discovery, no puni-tive damages, no appeal to a higher court and perhaps, most im-portantly, no publicity. Arbitration is not a public proceeding and creates no public record. It is the dream venue of the side in power, which is another way to say the side most likely to get sued. You rarely read about lawyers suing their clients except to collect a fee.

What to do? If it is what you prefer, ask that the arbitration clause be removed. The agreement will already have an exception that if the law firm decides to sue you for its fee, the firm gets to go court. Just ask that the document be reciprocal and you get to go to court if you sue the law firm. Or, it is equally reciprocal that the document says nothing about anyone suing anyone. Your entirely reasonable position is that you want nothing more than the law firm wants. Do not feel funny about bringing up such negative outcomes at the beginning of a relationship. The engagement letter is the moral equivalent of a prenuptial agreement, just dealing with the ugly stuff now so it is not so ugly later on. And, of course, the law firm is the side that first brought the issue up.

T he letter will show a sliding scale of billing rates for the lead attorney, junior attorney and legal assistant. Some legal en-deavors are on a flat fee, frequently found in estate planning, or a contingency fee (usually one third of the recovery, with you paying all the costs out of your share) normally found in personal injury. In those cases, the billing aspects are controlled. But in "uncon-trolled" billing there are still some controls you can exercise. For example, there is no charge to talk about certain topics and no bills over a certain amount per month.

Most people will never deal with any conflict with their lawyer, arbitration or not, but everyone will intently review their billing statement and many will show surprise. Items you might suggest to your attorney before you sign the engagement letter are:

- There is no charge to discuss purely clerical items such as your call to confirm an appointment or a court date. Believe it or not some lawyers consider all client contact as billable.
- No charge to discuss billing.
- No charge for costs such as photocopies or postage, or no charge unless those costs exceed $50.00 per month.
- No bills over a certain amount per month without authorization to avoid surprises.
- Recite back to the lawyer everything she said during the initial interview that you found to be important but was not contained in the letter. E.g., Good faith attempt to return all telephone calls within twenty-four hours, friendly staff, estimates of ultimate cost, working dates. If the lawyer says that she will have paperwork to you within two weeks of beginning, then put it in the letter. Write down everything that caused you to choose this lawyer over the others. It's good for the lawyer to understand these points and your thinking.

Once the letter reflects all that you want from the attorney, sign it, keep a copy and send it back with your check.

HOW TO FIRE YOUR LAWYER

Time and time again I have seen clients paralyzed over a wanting to leave the lawyer they have hired. In particular, they worry about how to fire him or her, as well as whether or not firing will work out successfully. They fear, per Mr. Shakespeare, that it is better to "Bear those ills we have rather than fly to others we know not of." Begin by hashing it out with a friend.

First you should be able to itemize in writing the list of dissatisfactions. Write them down. For example, he does not promptly return calls; I am always talking to the assistant and can never seem to get the lawyer; bills much higher than anticipated or discussed; is not following the terms of the engagement letter that I added; is arrogant, condescending, acts as if I work for him and not the other way around; seems uncomfortable with this area of the law; seems intimidated by opposing counsel, etc. Once you have listed your frustrations, show the list to someone who will tell you the truth. Are they legitimate reasons to fire your lawyer or do they spill over into whining? Are the expectations reasonable and anticipated by both the lawyer and the client? Would both the lawyer and the client agree that the expectations were fair? Is this really about the lawyer or is the client so emotionally involved in the case that he cannot see clearly? Does the client seek revenge or emotional vindication not money? Should the lawyer be fired or the client get counseling?

If the friend agrees that the lawyer should be fired and if you, the client, believe your friend is not just appeasing you, then find the lawyer who will be the successor to your current counsel. Ask a friend or relative to recommend a lawyer. Have a conversation, preferably in person, with the new lawyer, explain the situation, read your list of dissatisfactions and then listen carefully and observe the body language. If the new lawyer starts to squirm over your complaints then maybe you should stick with what you know. Lawyers are superb at analyzing whether you have a sound working relationship or not. Most importantly, can you do better? In several areas of law, the standard personality of the lawyer is the standard personality. Divorce comes to mind. A person does not choose to be a divorce lawyer unless she has a particular personality; a particular way of looking at life; and a particular ability to compartmentalize a hundred emotionally charged situations going on in her business life. Such a person, as Mr. Rudyard Kipling noted, "can keep [her] head when all about [her] are losing theirs and blaming it on [her]."

The point is that if you have a divorce lawyer and you are just going to get another standard divorce lawyer, why bother?

A subtle but crucial consideration is that in many criminal cases the law will give you only one free mistake, and the same is true with the number of successive lawyers you have on a particular case. Lawyer Number Two better be a home run because the system will effectively reduce your options for lawyer Number Three.

From the point of view of lawyer Number Two, you will be immediately suspect in your dissatisfaction with lawyer Number One. This has nothing to do with whether Two knows or has ever heard of One. The practice of law viewed as a fraternal, collegial organization died many years ago when it was replaced by avarice. The only exception to this continues in small communities. You will be suspect because Two will mentally put herself in One's position. For Two this situation is not insurmountable, but it is a caution. She will listen closely to your rationale for wanting to dismiss One.

If you skipped the steps of discussing Lawyer One with a friend, the potential Lawyer Number Two can double as your independent resource but she also has an interest that an independent lawyer in an unrelated field does not. And a key to whether Two will take you on is whether you have paid, or sincerely intend to pay, your final bill to Number One in full. Clients will mention to Two that their dissatisfaction with One is so severe that they do not intend to pay the final bill to One. A client will even think it is an incentive to Two to tell her that the money that would have been One's final payment will now be Two's retainer. While avarice is an unchanging barometer of human behavior, this instance has deeper currents. Number Two wants a client who is religious in her payments to lawyers and sees a gaping flaw in a client who enumerates reasons not to pay a lawyer, any lawyer. The girlfriend of a married man, who after the divorce becomes Wife Number Two, should understand that it is demonstrably within her husband's character to cheat and remarry. She may become the predecessor to Wife Number Three under identical circumstances down the road.

Lawyer Number Two does not wish to play that game and will find the client character flaw of using payment for services as a tool to be sufficient reason to not want to represent that client. Every lawyer who has practiced for any period of time has met the client who has gone from lawyer to lawyer, invariably not paying the previous lawyer's final bill. This client always has a reason why he is justified in not paying and yet continues to hire lawyers that after a time seem to justify the client's moving on.

Unless money is literally no object, after Lawyer Two the client will find it increasingly difficult to find another lawyer if Two does not work out. Lawyer radar locks on to any client with two previous lawyers unless one of them died. That client comes to the table with the invisible mark of danger and is not worth the risk. Dear client, Two better be perfect, or you will need a really good reason to look for Three because your selection is going to dwindle. The relationship will become much more about what lawyer will take you as opposed to your choice of which person you want.

Now, having made your way through the decision hurdles (which in real life is accomplished in a few days to two weeks) you may terminate Lawyer One with extreme prejudice. The non-confrontational way is to send a note with your last payment stating that you no longer wish to use One's services and to send your file (not a copy as we discussed) over to Lawyer Two. If you handle it this way, do not be surprised if you receive a call from One asking what happened. Be prepared with what you intend to say and be sincere without being accusatory. Keep in mind that as in many divorces, fault lies on both sides, although unlike marriage, in the legal relationship the primary burden of communication is on the attorney.

The more courageous approach is to call the lawyer and tell her why you are leaving. It may well be beneficial to her if she is willing to pay attention and learn. If she offers to waive a portion of or your entire final bill, then you are parting company with a fine human being regardless of legal performance.

Do not worry that the lawyer will argue with you to attempt to keep the relationship. We understand once the client expresses the desire to move on, that the relationship is over. At that point, the lawyer does not want to work with you any more than you want to work with her. This is not a complete rule, but by and large your parting conversation will be very short by mutual unspoken agreement.

Now you are free. Go and sin no more.

THE LAW ON THE MOON

One day Louis L'Amour, the Western author, was speeding along at the typewriter when his young daughter, Angelique, asked, *Daddy, why are you writing so fast?* Louis replied, *Because I want to see how the story turns out.*

That answer makes no sense and yet is wonderfully intuitive to the point of magical. I have felt the same way about *Games Lawyers Play*. I have wondered for a long time how it would turn out, how it would end. Until recently it did not matter because I was not at the end. This is the end. This is the essence of my observation from forty years in the practice. And this then is my distillation of where that observation has led me. How the story ends, appears as the answer to the question, "What is the law on the Moon?"

THE LAW ON THE MOON

James is an astronaut on the Moon exploring potential village sites just in case climate change is real. He is with his companion astronaut, Abigail. While on a hike together James makes a remark that Abigail does not like. So, she strikes his helmet with her gloved hand. The blow causes James' helmet to almost dislodge, which potentially could have killed him. He is sorely tempted to strike Abigail back on her helmet. Has Abigail committed a crime? By whose law? If James strikes back can he claim self-defense? He has heard about something called the Make My Day law. James' space suit is kind of like a home on the Moon and so maybe Abigail attempted a home invasion.

As James ponders the situation, he is not sure what constitutes a "day" on the Moon if he is always on the sunny side. He could call his lawyer and ask her, but would her hourly rate be at Earth hours or Moon hours? If James does not pay, how will she collect?

To compound it, Abigail is from Australia and James is from Malaysia. They rode in a Russian spacecraft funded by the United States. Which country's law controls? What if the colony they are founding on the Moon, breaks away from Earth and develops its own laws. Will those laws be retroactive to this incident? What is the Moon date of this incident?

What is the law on the Moon?

Let's begin with the aphorism *The Law is the Law*. We have all heard those words. Maybe we have even used them. Typically, we use them to get someone else to obey and not ask questions. They are just the grown-up version of Mom's, *Because I said so.* The words carry an unspoken moral imperative that there are certain laws that are universal and beyond debate. We may even agree that those laws are *The Law*. We just don't know exactly what we are agreeing to. A universal law would clearly be the law on the Moon. Does that include, *Because I said so?*

What is the law on the Moon?

The answer is the law, which is *The Law*, on the Moon is the same as the law on Mars and the law on Earth and the law in the Sirius star system. It is the law of everywhere and every time and every place and is not subject to change or interpretation or revision or revocation or meddling or overriding. We live those laws right now. We cannot hide from those laws and we cannot fool them. We cannot cease to live them. But what are they?

Seemingly three categories of laws compete to set our standards and values:

1. Laws of Government.
2. Laws of Religion.
3. Laws of personal Moral Code or conscience.

Most of us abdicate any conflict among the three categories and go for the safe bet which is that government law always controls, with religion in second place and conscience last. We may not believe that ranking in our heart of hearts, but it is a ranking that recognizes the relative severity of punishments if we fail to obey. Disobeying government is a clear and present danger. Disobeying religion is a clear danger but not a present one. Disobeying conscience is murky and can be compartmentalized out of the clear or present.

But for James and Abigail on the Moon, that ranking loses much of its fear-based power. We have seen that the laws of government do not easily function in the astronauts' situation and they each have very disparate religious beliefs, so they will not work. Finally, conscience was no help in preventing Abigail from striking James' helmet or him from desiring retaliation. Is there a higher awareness or are we stuck with the categories that have given us our earthly standards?

I suggest there are, in addition, and perhaps in preference, three laws that function as the laws or truths of everywhere.

THE LAWS OF THE MOON (and everywhere else) ARE:

I. WE ARE ALL ONE. THERE IS ONLY ONE OF US. EVERYTHING WITHIN THAT ONE IS INTERRELATED.

II. SURVIVAL IS NOT OUR BASIC INSTINCT. THE EXPRESSION OF DIVINITY IS OUR BASIC INSTINCT.

III. ALL CONDUCT IS BASED ON TWO EMOTIONS, LOVE AND FEAR. IN THE END, THERE IS ONLY LOVE BECAUSE FEAR IS THE REACTION TO THE ABSENCE OF LOVE.

We cannot fool these three laws. If we say that we intend to live by any of them, the Universe will test us for sincerity. We have all experienced taking an altruistic position and immediately being put to the test of how long we can maintain that position. The three are the laws we were born with and will die with, wherever in the Universe we are located

The core adversary of the three laws is "self-importance." Controlling self-importance understandably feels like a mere aphorism, as in remember your mother's birthday or understanding that too much pride is not good. It feels like something that it would be nice to strive for, not on a par with the Three Laws.

The answer is that self-importance directly conflicts with all three laws, but especially Number I, We Are All One. The logic underpinning the conflict, without getting too cute, is simple. A thing (us) cannot be superior to itself. We cannot be superior to ourselves since we are all one, I cannot be superior to you or anyone else. Hence self-importance is a black hole of misunderstanding of who we are in relation to the Universe and each other. Self-importance is a huge waste of emotional energy. Think how much energy we consume in our daily lives in a never ending state of being offended by the deeds and misdeeds of our fellow humans: government, family, politics, religion, schools, traffic....traffic.... traffic. Self-importance leaves us spending much of our lives offended by someone or some group. It also forces us to believe that we are in competition with our self, fictionalized as "others". The result is a life of endless need in the belief that there is not enough. That belief causes us compete with others for whatever there is not enough of: love, money, sex, property, food, warmth, power, roads with no traffic, etc. The belief empowers a cascading misdirected fantasy life all stemming from the misunderstanding that we are not all one, and to succeed we must be important, more important than another.

Much of the practice of law is built on the myth of self-importance. Much of the Games Lawyers Play stories have the personality flaws of their characters rooted in self-importance: the shoplifter, the bill collector, the second spouse, the divorcing couple, the needy child within us. Some of us get so offended we decide that we need a lawyer. Some of us become lawyers. On a deep level lawyers understand that their careers exist because of self-importance.

Self-importance is an energy sapping enemy. Self-importance made Abigail hit James. Self-importance made James want to hit her back and then figure out a law that would justify his conduct and prosecute her conduct on the Moon. If neither James nor Abigail had self-importance but instead self-respect while defining Self in its largest possible definition of We Are All One, then I would have been out of a job for the last 40 years and the world would as the commercial said, Live As One.

Distinct nations of people already exist who have lived variations of the Three Laws as a basic philosophy of life. They are the indigenous peoples, the first peoples, the Navajo Nation, the Sioux Nation, the Iroquois Nation in North America and others, such as the Aborigines of Australia, around the world, We have considered them primitive and instead we are primitive. Their laws functioned well for centuries. Ours flail. The proof of the inadequacy of our laws is that we are constantly changing them, as if through change we will eventually hit on the right answer.

The indigenous peoples have an underlying formula for a way of life based upon the first law. The Law of One. We should two.

None of the principles in this chapter is a surprise. You have heard all, or a variation of all, before. But what you have not heard is that the laws and the principles are not mere aphorisms, not mere modes of behavior to aspire to model. We are living by these laws right now. We have always lived by these laws. We will always live by these laws. No legislature can alter them. When the words "Denver" and "Colorado" and the "United States" and "Australia" and "Asia" no longer have meaning, when no one can remember ever having even heard those words, these laws will remain our law. These are the laws on the Moon. We can live with them, we can struggle against them or, as most of us, we can act in ignorance of them and wonder why we get divorced, get arrested, conflict with our step-mother or step-children, become a collection agent, become a victim or become a lawyer, all instead of just becoming a superb human who understands and lives: We Are All

One; The Expression Of Divinity Is Our Basic Instinct; and, Love Is All That Truly Exists.

Always Walk in Beauty.
David M. Cook

ACKNOWLEDGMENTS

I thank my Warrior Goddess wife, Jill Klancke, and my daughters, Michelle, Alexandra, Kaitlin and Halley for patiently, yet relentlessly, teaching me what it means to live love.

I humbly acknowledge the thousands of people who have permitted me the opportunity and honor to work with them and, to the extent of my ability, help them along their journey. I could not have seen nor understood the art of being human without them.

Finally, I thank my father, Mike Cook, who from my earliest age taught me to not merely observe people I meet along the way, but to seek to understand them. To realize life is not, "There but for the grace of God go I", but rather "There go I."

ABOUT THE AUTHOR

David M. Cook is an attorney, speaker and writer. He is on the board of the nonprofit The Tipi Raisers, working with the Lakota Sioux on Pineridge Indian Reservation and has previously served on, and then as chairman of, the board of directors of a national nonprofit for the developmentally disabled

David has won several editorial writing awards while owner of a western Colorado newspaper and presently speaks throughout Colorado, presenting "MOM ALWAYS LOVED YOU BEST", an insightful look at family behavior when death and dying of a parent are involved. He maintains an active legal practice in Denver, Colorado with his wife, and law partner, Jill.

David has four adult daughters and lives with his wife, two dogs, two birds and Myrtle the turtle. When not working, speaking or writing, David fly fishes and explores the remote southwest.

www.ingramcontent.com/pod-product-compliance
Lightning Source LLC
Chambersburg PA
CBHW021927190326
41519CB00009B/931